JUNIOR HIGH • MIDDLE SCHOOL

TALKSHEETS

—Updated!

50
CREATIVE DISCUSSIONS FOR
JUNIOR HIGH YOUTH GROUPS

DAVID LYNN

ZONDERVAN™

GRAND RAPIDS, MICHIGAN 49530 USA

Youth Specialties

www.youthspecialties.com

Youth Specialties

Junior High–Middle School TalkSheets—Updated! 50 creative discussions for junior high youth groups
Copyright © 2001 by David Lynn

Youth Specialties books, 300 S. Pierce St., El Cajon, CA 92020, are published by Zondervan, 5300 Patterson Ave. S.E., Grand Rapids, MI 49530.

Library of Congress Cataloging-in-Publication Data

Lynn, David, 1954-
    Junior high/middle school talksheets—updated! : 50 creative discussion starters for
youth groups / David Lynn.
       p. cm. — (TalkSheets series)
    ISBN-10: 0-310-23855-2
    ISBN-13: 978-0-310-23855-3
     1. Church group work with teenagers. 2. Junior high school students—Religious life. 3.
Middle school students—Religious life. I. Title. II. Series.

BV4447 .L9612 2001
286'.433—dc21

00-043941

Web site addresses listed in this book were current at the time of publication, but we can't guarantee they're still operational. If you have trouble with an URL, please contact us via e-mail (YS@YouthSpecialties.com) to let us know if you've found the current or new URL or if the URL is no longer operational.

Edited by Mary Fletcher, Anita Palmer, and Tamara Rice
Designed by PAZ Design Group
Illustrations and borders by Rick Sealock
Printed in the United States of America

08 09 10 11 12 • 19 18 17 16 15

CONTENTS

JUNIOR HIGH • MIDDLE SCHOOL
TALKSHEETS
—Updated!

THE HOWS AND WHATS OF TALKSHEETS

You are holding a very valuable book! No, it won't make you a genius or millionaire. But it does contain 50 instant discussions for junior high and middle school kids. Inside you'll find reproducible TalkSheets that cover a variety of hot topics—plus simple, step-by-step instructions on how to use them. All you need is this book, a few copies of the handouts, and some kids (and maybe a snack or two). You're on your way to landing on some serious issues in kids' lives today.

These TalkSheets are user-friendly and very flexible. They can be used in a youth group meeting, a Sunday school class, or a Bible study group. You can adapt them for either large or small groups. And, they can be covered in only 20 minutes as well as more intensively in two hours.

You can build an entire youth group meeting around a single TalkSheet, or you can use TalkSheets to supplement other materials and resources you might be using. These are tools for you—how you use them is your choice.

Junior High–Middle School TalkSheets— Updated! is not your average curriculum or workbook. This collection of discussions will get your kids involved and excited about talking through important issues. The TalkSheets deal with key topics and include interesting activities, challenging questions, and eye-catching graphics. They will challenge your kids to think about opinions, learn about themselves, and grow in their faith.

LEADING A TALKSHEET DISCUSSION

TalkSheets can be used as a curriculum for your youth group, but they are designed to be springboards for discussion. They encourage your kids to take part and interact with each other while talking about real life issues. And hopefully they'll do some serious thinking, discover new ideas for themselves, defend their points of view, and make decisions.

Youth today face a world of moral confusion. Youth leaders must teach the church's beliefs and values—and also help young people make the right choices in a world with so many options. Teenagers are bombarded with the voices of society and media messages—most of which drown out what they hear from the church.

A TalkSheet discussion works for this very reason. While dealing with the questions and activities on the TalkSheet, your kids will think carefully about issues, compare their beliefs and values with others, and make their own choices. TalkSheets will challenge your group to explain and rework their ideas in a Christian atmosphere of acceptance, support, and growth.

The most common fear of junior high and middle school youth group leaders is, "What will I do if the kids in my group just sit there and don't say anything?" Well, when kids don't have anything to say, it's because they haven't had a chance or time to get their thoughts organized! Most young people haven't developed the ability to think on their feet. Since many are afraid they might sound stupid, they don't know how to voice their ideas and opinions.

The solution? TalkSheets let your kids deal with the issues in a challenging, non-threatening way before the actual discussion begins. They'll have time to organize their thoughts, write them down, and ease their fears about participating. They may even look forward to sharing their answers! Most importantly, they'll (most likely) want to find out what others said and open up to talk through the topics.

If you're still a little leery about the success of a real discussion among your kids, that's okay! The only way to get them rolling is to get them started.

YOUR ROLE AS THE LEADER

The best discussions don't happen by accident. They require careful preparation and a sensitive leader. Don't worry if you aren't experienced or don't have hours to prepare.

TalkSheets are designed to help even the novice leader! The more TalkSheet discussions you lead, the easier it becomes. Keep the following tips in mind when using the TalkSheets as you get your kids talking.

BE CHOOSY

Each TalkSheet deals with a different topic. Choose a TalkSheet based on the needs and the maturity level of your group. Don't feel obligated to use the TalkSheets in the order they appear in this book. Use your best judgment and mix them up however you want—they are tools for you!

TRY IT YOURSELF

Once you have chosen a TalkSheet for your group, answer the questions and do the activities yourself. Imagine your kids' reactions to the TalkSheet. This will help you prepare for the discussion and understand what you are asking them to do. Plus, you'll have some time to think of other appropriate questions, activities, and Bible verses.

GET SOME INSIGHT

On each leader's guide page, you'll find numerous tips and ideas for getting the most out of your discussion. You may want to add some of your own thoughts or ideas in the margins. And, there's room to keep track of the date and the name of your group at the top of the leader's page. You'll also find suggestions for additional activities and discussion questions.

There are some references to Internet links throughout the TalkSheets. These are guides for you to find the resources and information that you need. For additional help, be sure to visit the Youth Specialties Web site at www.YouthSpecialties.com for information on materials and further links to finding what you need.

MAKE COPIES

Kids will need their own copy of the TalkSheet. Only make copies of the student's side of the TalkSheet! The material on the reverse side (the leader's guide) is just for you. You're able to make copies for your group because we've given you permission to do so. U.S. copyright laws have not changed, and it is still mandatory to request permission from a publisher before making copies of other published material. It is against the law not to do so. However, permission is given for you to make copies of this material for your group only, not for every youth group in your state. Thank you for cooperating.

INTRODUCE THE TOPIC

It's important to introduce the topic before you pass out the TalkSheets to your group. Depending on your group, keep it short and to the point. Be careful not to over-introduce the topic, sound preachy, or resolve the issue before you've started. Your goal is to spark their interest and leave plenty of room for discussion.

The best way to do this is verbally. You can tell a story, share an experience, or describe a situation or problem having to do with the topic. You might want to jump-start your group by asking something like, "What is the first thing you think of when you hear the word _____ [insert the topic]?" Then, after a few answers have been given, you can add something like, "Well, it seems we all have different ideas about this subject. Tonight we're going to investigate it a bit further..." Then pass out the TalkSheet and be sure that everyone has a pencil or pen. Now you're on your way! The following are excellent methods you can use to introduce any topic in this book—

- Show a related short film or video.
- Read a passage from a book or magazine that relates to the subject.
- Play a popular CD that deals with the topic.
- Perform a short skit or dramatic presentation.
- Play a simulation game or role-play, setting up the topic.
- Present current statistics, survey results, or read a current newspaper article that provides recent information about the topic.
- Use a crowd breaker or game, getting into the topic in a humorous way. For example if the topic is fun, play a game to begin the discussion. If the topic is success, consider a

game that helps the kids experience success or failure.

- Use posters, videos, or any other visuals to help focus attention on the topic.

There are endless possibilities for an intro—you are limited only by your own creativity! Each TalkSheet offers a few suggestions, but you are free to use any method with which you feel most comfortable. But do keep in mind that the introduction is a very important part of each session.

SET BOUNDARIES

It'll be helpful to set a few ground rules before the discussion. Keep the rules to a minimum, of course, but let the kids know what's expected of them. Here are suggestions for some basic ground rules—

- **What is said in this room stays in this room.** Emphasize the importance of confidentiality. Some kids will open up, some won't. Confidentiality is vital for a good discussion. If your kids can't keep the discussion in the room, then they won't open up.
- **No put-downs.** Mutual respect is important. If your kids disagree with some opinions, ask them to comment on the subject (but not on the other person). It's okay to attack the ideas, but not other people.
- **There is no such thing as a dumb question.** Your group members must feel free to ask questions at any time. The best way to learn is to ask questions and get answers.
- **No one is forced to talk.** Let everyone know they have the right to pass or not answer any question.
- **Only one person speaks at a time.** This is a mutual respect issue. Everyone's opinion is worthwhile and deserves to be heard.

Communicate with your group that everyone needs to respect these boundaries. If you sense that your group members are attacking each other or getting a negative attitude during the discussion, do stop and deal with the problem before going on.

ALLOW ENOUGH TIME

Pass out copies of the TalkSheet to your kids after the introduction and make sure that each person has a pen or pencil and a Bible. There are usually five or six activities on each TalkSheet. If your time

is limited, or if you are using only a part of the TalkSheet, tell the group to complete only the activities you'd like them to.

Decide ahead of time whether or not you would like the kids to work on the TalkSheets individually or in groups.

Let them know how much time they have for completing the TalkSheet and let them know when there is a minute (or so) left. Go ahead and give them some extra time and then start the discussion when everyone seems ready to go.

SET THE STAGE

Create a climate of acceptance. Most teenagers are afraid to voice their opinions because they don't want to be laughed at or look stupid in front of their peers. They want to feel safe if they're going to share their feelings and beliefs. Communicate that they can share their thoughts and ideas—even if they may be different or unpopular. If your kids get put-downs, criticism, laughter, or snide comments (even if their statements are opposed to the teachings of the Bible) it'll hurt the discussion.

Always phrase your questions—even those that are printed on the TalkSheets—so that you are asking for an opinion, not an answer. For example if a question reads, "What should Bill have done in that situation?" change it to, "What do you think Bill should have done in that situation?" The simple addition of the three words "do you think" makes the question less threatening and a matter of opinion, rather than a demand for the right answer. Your kids will relax when they will feel more comfortable and confident. Plus, they'll know that you actually care about their opinions and they'll feel appreciated!

LEAD THE DISCUSSION

Discuss the TalkSheet with the group and encourage all your kids to participate. Communicate that it's important for them to respect each other's opinions and feelings! The more they contribute, the better the discussion will be.

If your youth group is big, you may divide it into smaller groups of six to 12. Each of these small groups should have a facilitator—either an adult leader or a student member—to keep the discussion going. Remind the facilitators not to dominate the others. If the group looks to the facilitator for an answer, ask him or her to direct the questions or responses back to the group. Once the smaller groups have completed their discussions, combine them into one large group and ask the different groups to share their ideas.

You don't have to divide the groups up with every TalkSheet. For some discussions, you may want to vary the group size and or divide the meeting into groups of the same sex.

The discussion should target the questions and answers on the TalkSheet. Go through them one at a time and ask the kids to share their responses. Have them compare their answers and brainstorm new ones in addition to the ones they've written down. Encourage them to share their opinions and answers, but don't force those who are quiet.

AFFIRM ALL RESPONSES—RIGHT OR WRONG

Let your kids know that their comments and contributions are appreciated and important. This is especially true for those who rarely speak up in group activities. Make a point of thanking them for joining in. This will be an incentive for them to participate further.

Remember that affirmation doesn't mean approval. Affirm even those comments that seem wrong to you. You'll show that everyone has a right to express their ideas—no matter how controversial they may be. If someone states an opinion that is off base, make a mental note of the comment. Then in your wrap-up, come back to the comment or present a different point of view in a positive way. But don't reprimand the student who voiced the comment.

DON'T BE THE AUTHORITATIVE ANSWER

Some kids think you have the right answer to every question. They'll look to you for approval, even when they are answering another group member's question. If they start to focus on you for answers, redirect them toward the group by making a comment like, "Remember that you're talking to everyone, not just me."

Your goal as the facilitator is to keep the discussion alive and kicking. It's important that your kids think of you as a member of the group—on their level. The less authoritative you are, the

more value your own opinions will have. If your kids view you as a peer, they will listen to your comments. You have a tremendous responsibility to be, with sincerity, their trusted friend.

LISTEN TO EACH PERSON

God gave you one mouth and two ears. Good discussion leaders know how to listen. Although it's tempting at times, don't monopolize the discussion. Encourage others to talk first—then express your opinions during your wrap-up.

DON'T FORCE IT

Encourage all your kids to talk, but don't make them comment. Each member has the right to pass. If you feel that the discussion isn't going well, go on to the next question or restate the question to keep them moving.

DON'T TAKE SIDES

You'll probably have different opinions expressed in the group from time to time. Be extra careful not to take one side or another. Encourage both sides to think through their positions—ask questions to get them deeper. If everyone agrees on an issue, you can play devil's advocate with tough questions and stretch their thinking. Remain neutral—your point of view is your own, not that of the group.

DON'T LET ANYONE (INCLUDING YOU) TAKE OVER

Nearly every youth group has one person who likes to talk and is perfectly willing to express an opinion on any subject. Try to encourage equal participation from all the kids.

SET UP FOR THE TALK

Make sure that the seating arrangement is inclusive and encourages a comfortable, safe atmosphere for discussion. Theater-style seating (in rows) isn't discussion-friendly. Instead, arrange the chairs in a circle or semicircle (or on the floor with pillows!).

LET THEM LAUGH!

Discussions can be fun! Most of the TalkSheets include questions that'll make them laugh and get them thinking, too.

LET THEM BE SILENT

Silence can be a scary for discussion leaders! Some react by trying to fill the silence with a question or a comment. The following suggestions may help you to handle silence more effectively—

- Be comfortable with silence. Wait it out for 30 seconds or so to respond. You may want to restate the question to give your kids a gentle nudge.
- Talk about the silence with the group. What does the silence mean? Do they really not have any comments? Maybe they're confused, embarrassed, or don't want to share.
- Answer the silence with questions or comments like, "I know this is challenging to think about..." or "It's scary to be the first to talk." If you acknowledge the silence, it may break the ice.
- Ask a different question that may be easier to handle or that will clarify the one already posed. But don't do this too quickly without giving them time to think the first one through.

KEEP IT UNDER CONTROL

Monitor the discussion. Be aware if the discussion is going in a certain direction or off track. This can happen fast, especially if the kids disagree or things get heated. Mediate wisely and set the tone that you want. If your group gets bored with an issue, get them back on track. Let the discussion unfold, but be sensitive to your group and who is or is not getting involved.

If a student brings up a side issue that's interesting, decide whether or not to purse it. If discussion is going well and the issue is worth discussion, let them talk it through. But, if things get way off track, say something like, "Let's come back to that subject later if we have time. Right now, let's finish our discussion on..."

BE CREATIVE AND FLEXIBLE

You don't have to follow the order of the questions on the TalkSheet. Follow your own creative in-stinct. If you find other ways to use the TalkSheets, use them! Go ahead and add other questions or Bible references.

Don't feel pressured to spend time on every single activity. If you're short on time, you can skip some items. Stick with the questions that are the most interesting to the group.

SET YOUR GOALS

TalkSheets are designed to move along toward a goal, but you need to identify your goal in advance. What would you like your young people to learn? What truth should they discover? What is the goal of the session? If you don't know where you're going, it's doubtful you will get there.

BE THERE FOR YOUR KIDS

Some kids may want to talk more with you (you got 'em thinking!). Let them know that you can talk one-on-one with them afterwards.

Communicate to the kids that they can feel free to talk with you about anything with confidentiality. Let them know you're there for them with support and concern, even after the TalkSheet discussion has been completed.

USE THE BIBLE

Most adults believe the Bible has authority over their lives. It's common for adults to start their discussions or to support their arguments with Bible verses. But today's teenagers form their opinions and beliefs from their own life situations first—then they decide how the Bible fits their needs. TalkSheets start with the realities of the adolescent world and then move toward the Bible. You'll be able to show them that the Bible can be their guide and that God does have something to say to them about their own unique situations.

The last activity on each TalkSheet uses Bible verses that were chosen for their application to each issue. But they aren't exhaustive. Feel free to add whatever other verses you think would fit well and add to the discussion.

After your kids read the verses, ask them to think how the verses apply to their lives and summarize the meanings for them. For example, after reading the passage for "Livin' It Up," you may summarize by saying something like, "See? God wants us to have fun! In fact, Jesus spoke in his parables of feasts, dancing, and celebration. It's obvious that God wants Christians to have good times—but to be careful, too."

CLOSE THE DISCUSSION

Present a challenge to the group by asking yourself, "What do I want the kids to remember most from this discussion?" There's your wrap-up! It's important to conclude by affirming the group and offering a summary that ties the discussion together.

Sometimes you won't need a wrap-up. You may want to leave the issue hanging and discuss it in another meeting. That way, your group can think about it more and you can nail down the final ideas later.

TAKE IT FURTHER

On the leader's guide page, you'll find additional discussion activities—labeled More—for following up on the discussion. These aren't a must, but highly recommended. They let the kids reflect upon, evaluate, review, and assimilate what they've learned. These activities may lead to more discussion and better learning.

After you've done the activity, be sure to debrief your kids on the activity, either now or at the next group meeting. A few good questions to ask about the activity are—

- What happened when you did this activity or discussion?

- Was it helpful or a waste of time?

- How did you feel when doing the activity or discussion?

- Did the activity/discussion make you think differently or affect you in any way?

- In one sentence state what you learned from this activity or discussion.

A FINAL WORD TO THE WISE — THAT'S YOU!

Some of these TalkSheets deal with topics that may be sensitive or controversial for your kids. Issues like sexuality or materialism aren't discussed openly in some churches. You're encouraging discussion and inviting your kids to express their opinions. As a result, you may be criticized by parents or others in your church who may not see the importance of such discussions. Use your best judgment. If you suspect that a particular TalkSheet will cause problems, you may not want to use it. Or you may want to tweak a particular TalkSheet and cover only some of the questions. Either way, the potential bad could outweigh the good—better safe than sorry. To avoid any misunderstanding, you may want to give the parents or senior pastor (or whoever else you are accountable to) copies of the TalkSheet before you use it. Let them know the discussion you would like to have and the goal you are hoping to accomplish. Challenge your kids to take their TalkSheet home to talk about it with their parents. How would their parents, as young people, have answered the questions? Your kids may find that their parents understand them better than they thought! Also, encourage them to think of other Bible verses or ways that the TalkSheet applies to their lives.

FEELING SMALL

1. Do you have a **nickname** your friends call you?
What is it?
How did you get the nickname?
How does it make you feel?

2. How would you feel?
If you thought everybody was laughing at you?
If you were a failure in front of your friends?
If you were different from everyone else your age?

3. It was a Friday and Jason got on the bus feeling really good. That night he was going to hang out and sleep over at his friend Bryan's house. It was going to be a great weekend. But when he got to school, things changed his good mood. In his first period math class, he found out that he flunked yesterday's quiz. To top it off, Bryan ignored him and cancelled their plans. Bryan was invited to Dawn's house for a party, and Jason hadn't been invited. Jason couldn't figure out what was wrong with him. He wondered if God cared—after all, didn't God want Jason to have fun?

Didn't God understand?

What advice do you have for Jason?

What would you say to Bryan if you were Jason?

Do you think God understands Jason's situation?

4. Do the statements below describe you? Write **Y (yes, that's me)** or **N (no, that's not me)**.
____ I feel good about who I am.
____ I often daydream I am someone else.
____ I have trouble making friends.
____ I feel I am just as important as anyone else at school.

____ I always compare myself to my friends.
____ Most people are smarter than I am.
____ I sometimes put other people down.
____ I feel left out sometimes.

5. Wanna know how much God thinks of you? Check out the following Bible verses and jot down what you think he says.

Psalm 139:13-14

Colossians 1:21-23

Matthew 18:12-14

FEELING SMALL [i n f e r i o r i t y]

THIS WEEK

Everyone has feelings of inferiority, but during the junior high and middle school years, these feelings are intensified. These feelings can be painful, especially among junior high or middle school aged kids, who are so heavily influenced by their peers. This session examines those feelings of rejection, hurt, and inferiority and gives you the opportunity to talk about these feelings in a warm, supportive Christian environment.

OPENER

When discussing inferiority, it is very important that the kids feel secure enough to talk. That means no put-downs!

Try the Gratitude Game. Ask a member of the group to come to the front or sit in a special chair. Then ask the group to brainstorm what things they would be thankful for, if they were the person selected. This can be very affirming for the group. Try it with several kids or all of them, if you have time.

THE DISCUSSION, BY THE NUMBERS

1. The purpose of this item is to get the kids to think about the nicknames others have given them and how they feel about them. Begin by sharing a nickname you had as a teen and how you felt about it. Then ask if anyone would be willing to share their nicknames and their feelings about them.

2. Make sure your kids have an opportunity to share their feelings without being afraid of being laughed at. You might want to share some of your own junior high and middle school experiences. Ask the kids to share some positive nicknames and experiences as well—times when they really felt affirmed, when people applauded them, or when they felt successful, proud, and accepted by others.

3. This tension-getter allows kids to role-play a counselor and give advice to someone else about feeling small. Let the kids brainstorm several choices Jason could make. Then illustrate how these ideas could apply to their own situations.

4. Choose two or three of the less threatening statements and ask for a show of hands to find out who checked Y (yes, that's me) or N (no, that's not me). Some won't want to share their answers. There aren't any right or wrong answers here, so try to keep the discussion flexible and focus on how the kids feel. During the wrap-up, you may want to go back to some of the statements and shed new light on their feelings.

5. The Bible passages listed give you an opportunity to focus the discussion on God's unconditional love and acceptance for us. You can guide the discussion toward God's feelings for us. You may want to focus your attention on Psalm 139:13-14. Then listen carefully to your kids as they share their paraphrases of the verses.

THE CLOSE

Help your kids understand that some feelings aren't either good or bad. Communicate to your kids that all feelings are natural and healthy—although some people think that certain feelings are sinful. Teenagers need to understand it's not the feeling itself, but what's done with the feeling that's sinful. When they feel down, they need to be careful not to do something they'll regret later. Feelings are temporary, but some consequences of sinful behavior will stick around forever.

Let the kids know that they are each a special, gifted person created in the image of God. It's important to let your youths know that everyone (including you, their parents, the senior pastor) feel inferior sometimes—it's normal! Even confident people who seem to have it all together feel insecure at times. Your kids shouldn't forget that God loves them—he's their biggest fan. If God has a wallet, their picture is in it! In fact, their names are engraved in the palm of his hand (Isaiah 49:16).

Challenge your kids to accept God's love and forgiveness, even when they don't feel loved or forgiven. God is always there for them, no matter how they feel about themselves.

MORE

● Ask your kids to think of themselves as the following—
⇨ Any place in the world. What would they look like if they were a city, or an island in the middle of the ocean? What kinds of buildings, hills, valleys, roads (some under construction), or other areas of interest would be there? What would the map look like?
⇨ Any object in the world. What would they be if they were anything in the world? Why? What do they like or not like about what they chose?
⇨ A candy bar. What kind of candy bar would they be? Why?
⇨ A celebrity? What characteristics of the celebrity do they like? Why?
⇨ Any other examples that you'd like to add.
● Or your kids could bring a CD or video that best expresses how they feel when they feel inferior. Play the music or video and discuss how it describes their emotion. What does the music say about feeling small? What do people do when they feel inferior?

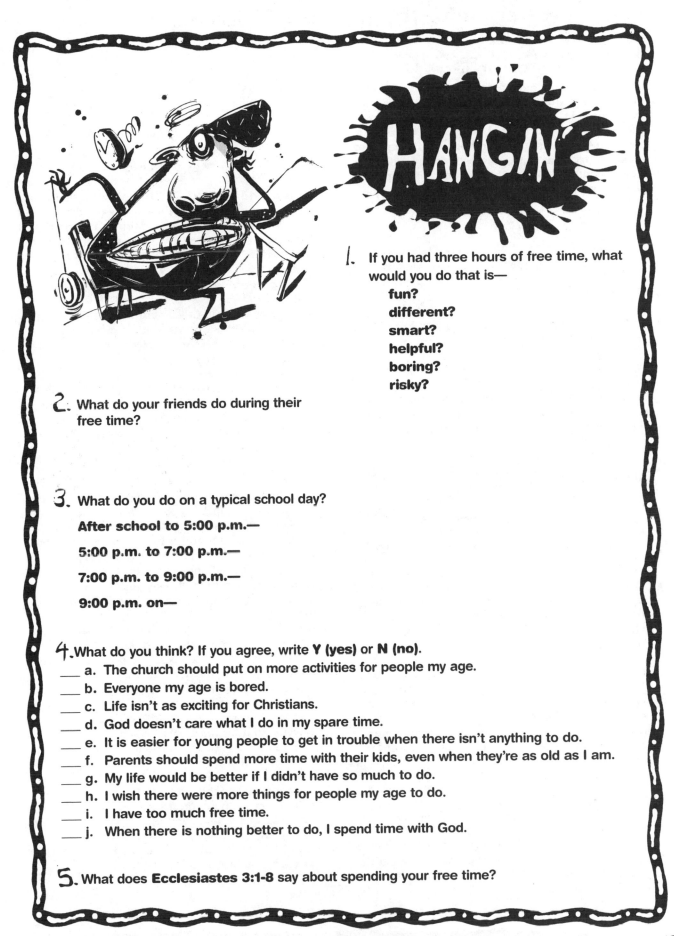

HANGIN

1. If you had three hours of free time, what would you do that is—
    fun?
    different?
    smart?
    helpful?
    boring?
    risky?

2. What do your friends do during their free time?

3. What do you do on a typical school day?

    After school to 5:00 p.m.—

    5:00 p.m. to 7:00 p.m.—

    7:00 p.m. to 9:00 p.m.—

    9:00 p.m. on—

4. What do you think? If you agree, write **Y (yes)** or **N (no)**.
    ___ a. The church should put on more activities for people my age.
    ___ b. Everyone my age is bored.
    ___ c. Life isn't as exciting for Christians.
    ___ d. God doesn't care what I do in my spare time.
    ___ e. It is easier for young people to get in trouble when there isn't anything to do.
    ___ f. Parents should spend more time with their kids, even when they're as old as I am.
    ___ g. My life would be better if I didn't have so much to do.
    ___ h. I wish there were more things for people my age to do.
    ___ i. I have too much free time.
    ___ j. When there is nothing better to do, I spend time with God.

5. What does **Ecclesiastes 3:1-8** say about spending your free time?

HANGIN' [free time]

THIS WEEK

Young people today have more freedom than they've ever had. Sure, there's more extracurricular activities to participate in, but the number of kids who come home from school to empty houses continues to grow. With more unsupervised time, kids have more freedom to try new things and experiment with new behaviors and identities. This session will help you and your group discuss how Christians can handle free time.

OPENER

For a smooth transition you may want to pass out pencils or pens and paper and ask your kids (without letting others see their answers) to complete the following sentences—

- If I had nothing to do for a whole day I would—
- When I have an extra hour, I like to—
- The best way for me to relax is to—
- When someone says free time I think of—

Now ask your kids to guess how others in your group may have completed the sentences. It's interesting to see what different people like to do with their free time.

THE DISCUSSION, BY THE NUMBERS

1. As your kids to share their responses, encourage creative thinking and ask for as many ideas as possible. List them on a sheet of poster board or whiteboard.

2. List the items and then have the kids rate each one (10 can be good, 1 can be bad). Or choose the best five and the worst five. It's important that the kids understand they have lots of choices for using free time—some good and some bad.

3. This will give your kids a look at how they spend a typical school day. You can do the same using a weekend, too. Focus on the fact that everyone has the same length of time every day, but each spends it differently. If some say that they get bored or have nothing to do, brainstorm other ways to use their time. Ask the kids to offer ideas and help each other.

4. This item should stimulate a lot of discussion. You may want to go over each of the statements and ask for opinions. Keep the discussion moving toward constructive decisions and actions. If the group agrees with a statement (like "Life isn't as exciting for Christians"), ask why they think that and what can be done.

5. This passage shows that everyone needs to balance their free time. Ask the group to share their sentences. Go through the passage and ask them to give modern day examples of activities from the passage.

THE CLOSE

Time is a gift from God—he doesn't want us to waste it. But he does want us to relax and enjoy ourselves, too. Encourage your kids to challenge themselves—to try a new activity, such as a playing a new sport, starting a new hobby, or volunteering. Challenge them to set a new goal for themselves and use part of their extra time to get to know God better.

You may want to talk about activities that are "builders" and those that aren't. For example, watching the same movie everyday after school won't let them try anything new or learn new things. But, what about surfing the Internet, trying a new sport, or helping their mom with their little brother? What is the difference between spending time that stimulates them and simply passes the time? How would God want them to spend our time and relax, too?

MORE

- If you're interested, plan a service project that you and your kids can do together after school or on a weekend. Examples may include visiting a rest home, collecting food for a food bank, performing yard work for the elderly, or raking leaves. Get everyone involved and then talk later with the group about the project. How did they feel while using their time for others? What difference did their time make to others?
- How do you and your kids spend your spare time? Ask your kids (and you, too) to journal their activities for a week or a weekend to see how they spend their time. Include everything—sleeping, eating, watching TV, helping out around home. Then, have them circle those things they did during their free time. What did they learn about how they spend their time. What would they like to change in the future? What did they spend the most time on and why?
- If your kids would like a part-time or after–school job, set up a job bank. You could match up kids with people in the church who need help with tasks such as housework, mowing lawns, washing cars, sweeping sidewalks, or taking inventory. Or you could auction off their services in a fundraiser for your group or an organization.

GREAT EXPECTATIONS

1. What are **three** words that you think describe the teenage years?

2. What is **one thing** that worries you about becoming a teenager?

3. What would you tell someone your age who—
   a. was having trouble making friends?
   b. couldn't get along with his or her parents?
   c. didn't like the way he or she looked?
   d. was trying to act older than he or she really is?
   e. wasn't doing well in school?
   f. was pressured into doing drugs by peers?

4. Below, write **Yeah!** for those that sound exciting and **Uh!** for those that don't.
   _____ Taking high school classes   _____ Going to parties
   _____ Getting a drivers license   _____ Going to a high school youth group
   _____ Getting a job   _____ Meeting new friends
   _____ Handling sexual pressures   _____ Deciding on college or a career
   _____ Dating   _____ Facing more responsibility
   _____ Getting more freedom from parents _____ Playing high school sports

5. Take a look at these verses—what do you think they say about the future?

   Psalm 119:9-10

   1 Timothy 4:12

   Titus 2:6-8

GREAT EXPECTATIONS [preparing for adolescence]

THIS WEEK

Teenagers today deal with rapid change, confusion, and stress. These factors—along with the other physical, emotional, and intellectual changes—make it hard for young people to cope. This session is designed to let your kids know that it's important to talk about the issues they face as they grow older. It encourages them to ask questions and share their worries and fears.

OPENER

Introduce this topic by having your kids suggest movies or TV shows about teenagers. Make a list of their choices and ask the student to decide if these programs or films deal with the issues in realistic ways or not. How do these shows portray teenagers?

You may also collect a stash of teen magazines (such as *Seventeen*, *Teen* or *YM*) and conduct a magazine scavenger hunt. Divide the group into teams and give each team a magazine. Then call out—or one of your kids call out—the name of something that's advertised (such as names of colognes, perfumes, cosmetics, or brand name clothing) a frequently used word (something you hear your kids use a lot!), a teenage actor, a specific movie title, and so on. The team that finds the item as quickly as possible magazine gets a point.

THE DISCUSSION, BY THE NUMBERS

1. Make a list of the words that the kids used to describe the teenage years. Take your time and focus on how your kids are feeling—fears, excitement, anxieties, et cetera. They most likely will have some misconceptions about the teenage years. There may be some other "red flag" words or phrases that catch your attention. Use this discussion to help them understand these assumptions and discover a healthier, more realistic expectation of teenagers.

2. You may want to rephrase the question with something like this, "What do you think worries other kids your age about becoming a teenager?" Keep a list of their responses on a whiteboard or poster board. Without glossing over their worries about teen-hood, let them know that their fears are very normal. Everyone—even their parents, teachers, and even you—worries about new experiences! Your kids will face many new ones as they enter their teen years. Encourage them to talk with you or another adult if they are anxious about specific issues and want more information or advice.

3. As your kids share their answers to this, ask them if they agree or disagree with the advice given.

Emphasize that it's important for them to support and encourage each other. Challenge them to find ways to build each other up—even if this means cutting the teasing and put-downs.

4. Here's your chance to talk about the expectations of high school. Discuss with them the pros and cons of growing up and what will change as they get older. Let them know you are there for them anytime to offer advice or answer questions that come up.

5. Encourage some of your kids to read their summaries aloud and work with them to make applications for their lives. A useful Bible verse for this is 1 Timothy 4:12.

THE CLOSE

The teenage years are filled with both exciting and confusing times. The fears and stress they face are understandable. There's no doubt that everyone will grow and change—in different ways and at different speeds—during this time. But these changes are exciting, too! You kids will face new challenges and adventures, experience new things, and learn about themselves. And, God is working through all this—molding each one into a different, more experienced, and changing person.

Take some time to talk about what fears they are dealing with and remind them that they come to you at any time with questions or concerns. And ask your kids what they think God feels about them as young people. Does God listen to them as much as their parents? Of course! He's there for them—listening to their fears and frustrations, any time, anywhere.

MORE

- Bank on some of your older high school kids or early college kids for a Q & A session with your junior highers or middle schoolers. Encourage them to ask them what it's like to be in high school, what it's like to be a Christian, how to get along with parents, how they deal with peer pressure, and so on. To keep things rolling smoothly, have your kids write out a few questions before the Q & A.

- Need a better activity for kids who are especially tactile or visual? Whether in a group or individually at home, ask your kids to cut pictures out of magazines—teen, sports, or whatever—that represent teenagers or portray adolescence. Then use them to create a collage that represents your kids' understanding of (or apprehensions about) becoming a teenager.

GOTTA GET TO SCHOOL

1. **What** is your favorite class in school?

   Why is it your favorite?

   Who is your favorite teacher?

   Why is he or she your favorite?

2. Place an **X** on the line below indicating how you feel about your relationship with God when you are at school.

   Close to God   **Far from God**

3. What do you think? Answer **Yeah (I agree)**, **Nah (I disagree)** or **Duh (I don't know)**.

   _____ If I don't get good grades, then I'm a failure.

   _____ I don't have Christian friends at school.

   _____ A person shouldn't be required to go to school.

   _____ I feel out of place at school.

   _____ People at school really care about my feelings.

   _____ What I learn at church helps me in school.

   _____ I wish I could go to another school.

   _____ People at school don't understand my Christian beliefs.

   _____ Most of my classes are a waste of time.

   _____ My school is really fun.

4. Flip to **Proverbs 9:10** and **Colossians 3:17** in your Bible. What do you think each verse means for your life?

GOTTA GET TO SCHOOL [s c h o o l]

THIS WEEK

Junior high and middle school kids spend most of their time in school. Some kids like it, some don't. But most fall somewhere in between. School is a crucial learning time—socially, academically, emotionally and physically. Just like adults have to do with their jobs, young people need a chance to vent their concerns and frustrations about school! This TalkSheet gives you a chance to listen to them and deal with their feelings about school.

OPENER

Write one (or more) of the following incomplete sentences on a whiteboard or large sheet of newsprint—

- If I could change on thing about my school, I would—
- What I like least about school is—
- A new subject that they should add in my school is—
- What makes school hard for me is—
- If I were a teacher in my school, I would—

After your group completes the sentence(s), make a master list of their answers. This activity should get them talking about their school experiences.

Another way is to start the session is with a pop quiz. Run the test like a teacher—no talking and no looking at others' papers. The quiz may cover a book of the Bible or whatever was discussed the week before. The kids will probably complain that this activity is "just like school"—bingo!

THE DISCUSSION, BY THE NUMBERS

1. As the student share their answers, find out why they chose the favorite classes they did. The second part of the question lets them brainstorm what they like about their favorite teachers. Be careful—you may learn something new about what teenagers want to see in adult leaders! Make a list of all the positive characteristics mentioned.

2. Many young kids have difficulty relating their Christian faith to their school. Some of them may want to share stories or experiences to show that being a Christian can be challenging at school. Those who attend Christian schools may have more or different frustrations. Let them feel free to vent these frustrations, but be careful not to compare Christian versus public or to take sides.

3. Spend some time discussing the first statement concerning grades. They may feel this pressure from parents, teachers, and other kids. Communicate that grades won't make or break you as a person—they do not prove intelligence, character, or success. In fact, there are several

famous and brilliant people who didn't do well in school! Although this isn't an excuse for slacking off in school, encourage them to always try their best and not to get hung up on grades.

4. Ask the kids how they'd apply this verse to education. Clarify that the "fear of God" doesn't mean being afraid of God, but it means having a close relationship with him. How can your kids learn about God while they are at school? What would God say about studying hard and getting good grades? How can they glorify God in their math class or on their basketball team?

THE CLOSE

School is an important time of preparation and growth. Education is so much more than just math, science, language, or whatever subjects! You may want to point out that they go to school to learn discipline (by going to school every day); self-respect and a sense of identity (by following through on assignments), work ethics (by working hard on projects), social skills (by interacting with their peers and teachers); and responsibility to God and others. Believe it or not, they are getting equipped for future success in high school, college, and their careers!

Challenge your kids to take their faith to school with them. Christianity isn't just a Sunday activity—it carries through the whole week. Discuss how other kids view them as Christians and how that affects them. Do they have both Christian and non-Christian friends at school? How can they affect non-Christians at school? Why is support important among other Christian kids?

MORE

- Experience junior high or middle school lunch in a cafeteria! (Watch out for the flying jello!) Go and have lunch with some of your kids at school. You'll step into their world and show them that you're interested in their school lives and learn more about them, too.

  Most schools have policies and rules about on-campus guests, so be sure to check in with the school principal or supervisor before you go or when you get there.

- Are exams stressing them out? You may like to host a group study session or study hall the next time your kids have exams. You can do this either on a Sunday afternoon or weekday evening (but clear it with parents first!). Keep your kids fueled up with some study snacks and a few short, study breaks.

AM I NORMAL?

1. What do you think is the **best** age to be?
   (circle one)
   2   5   10   13   16   18   21   30   45   65

2. Which one would you choose?
   I'm growing up—
   a. faster than most kids my age.
   b. about the same as others my age.
   c. not as fast as others my age.

3. If you could change **one thing** about yourself,
   what would it be?

4. How do you feel when you look in the mirror? **Circle** two of the following things.

worried	angry	embarrassed	special
proud	flawed	lonely	handsome
happy	shy	pretty	depressed

5. **Check** what you think are normal concerns for people your age.
   - ❏ Will someone want to date me?
   - ❏ Do others think I'm cool?
   - ❏ Do I have enough friends?
   - ❏ Am I attractive to the opposite sex?
   - ❏ Will my parents start trusting me?
   - ❏ All my friends are having sex—what about me?
   - ❏ How can I get better grades?
   - ❏ Does God think I'm okay?
   - ❏ I have no money...
   - ❏ Will I get accepted to college?
   - ❏ Can I survive high school?
   - ❏ Will I make the teams I try out for?
   - ❏ Should I drink or do drugs?
   - ❏ How do I live a Christian life?

6. Read the verses below and then draw a line between the verse and the correct description
   1. 2 Chronicles 34:1-2
   2. Luke 1:26-28
   3. Luke 2:51-52
   4. Luke 15:11-13
   5. 2 Timothy 3:15

   a. God was with her.
   b. He left his family and wanted his money.
   c. He knew Bible verses even as a child.
   d. Jesus grew up.
   e. He did the right thing in God's eyes.

AM I NORMAL? [g r o w i n g   u p]

THIS WEEK

Growing up can be hard! Everyone grows at a different rate and some kids they don't think they're normal. This discussion will give you a chance to talk about the ins and outs of growing up and how to deal with its stresses and pressures. You'll also be able to affirm your kids and challenge them to encourage and support each other.

OPENER

Got some extra preparation time? Videotape statements from some adults (such as people you work with, random people in the shopping mall, your pastor) talking about their own experiences or sharing stories of when they were junior high and middle school kids. Then show the video to your group to start the discussion—what did they think about what they heard and saw? What stories or examples did they like? Why or why not?

Not enough time? Have your kids bring in a picture of when they were a baby or small child. Mix the pictures up and post them on a poster board or whiteboard. Give each picture a number and have each kid guess who is who from the pictures. Whoever gets the most correct answers wins.

THE DISCUSSION, BY THE NUMBERS

1. Have your kids vote on their choice. Why did they choose this age? What is appealing to them about this age? What is scary about this age or another? You may want to talk about the different opportunities that come with each age and what's exciting or scary about those.

2. Point out to your kids that everyone grows at a different pace. During early adolescence, it is normal for some to mature as much as six years earlier than others! Girls mature physically much faster than boys do. Remind them that they are all unique—no one will grow and develop in the same way.

3. Let them know about you! Start the discussion with changes that happened to you when you were in junior high and middle school. Maybe tell them what you would like to change about yourself or are working on. Your kids may be hesitant to share their own changes—that's okay.

4. This will open up a discussion on self-image. From their responses, you'll be able to get a feel for the kids' self-esteem. You may want to share what your own self-image was as a teen and how you changed. What was hard for you? What made you grow and change? You may also wish to

collect their TalkSheets (unsigned) to read how each chose to answer this item.

5. Junior high and middle schoolers are particularly sensitive about fitting in, being normal, and going along with peers. Use these topics to talk about what is "normal." Youth today have far too many adult worries and responsibilities. In many ways, they've lost some of their childhood. Ask them to arrange these concerns into two categories—concerns to deal with now and concerns to deal with later in life. Encourage them to keep realistic expectations of themselves and others.

6. These Bible verses deal with growing up. Luke 2:51-52 is a useful passage to read and talk about Christ's childhood.

THE CLOSE

Point out that God does know what it's like to grow up—Jesus was once their age! He went through the same challenges and trials that your kids do. God understands all their fears and emotions because he created them and knows each one better than they know themselves.

Finally, some in your group may be dealing with some heavy adult issues for their age—abuse, depression, drugs, sexual activity, and more. Keep an ear out for these larger concerns. Some of your kids may be asking for your attention and help. If you sense that your kids are struggling, or if someone approaches you, encourage them to talk about their concerns with a trusted adult. The TalkSheets on suicide, anger, and premarital sex give more information and list Internet links for these issues.

MORE

- Go back in time and have your kids share memories of stories from when they were little. What was different when they were younger? Or have some share stories about their younger siblings—these can be quite funny. You may want to play a grown-up version of show and tell—something from when they were young that's extra special or memorable to them.
- Or ask your kids to make a giant collage that best describes how they feel as young people. This can include phrases, words, and pictures that describe people their age. And they write words or draw pictures that describe them as young people. You can either do this in the meeting as a group or have them put it together at home to share with the group later.

WWW.YOURFAMILY.COM

1. What are **three activities** that your family does together?

   Which one do you enjoy the most?

2. **Circle** three words that best describe your family.

fun	strange	peaceful	friendly
busy	close	strict	helpful
happy	Christian	boring	angry
embarrassing	changing	stressful	caring
loving	critical	noisy	loyal

3. If you could change **one thing** about your family, what would it be?

4. What would you like to **learn** more about? (check one or more)
   - ❏ How to get along better with my siblings
   - ❏ How to get my parents off my back
   - ❏ How to have more fun as a family
   - ❏ How to get along better with my parents
   - ❏ How to have a closer family
   - ❏ How to have family devotions
   - ❏ How to tell my parents how I really feel

5. God has a lot to say about families! Check out these verses and then write what each verse says about your family.

   Proverbs 6:20-22

   Romans 12:9-13

   Ephesians 6:1-4

WWW.YOURFAMILY.COM [family life]

THIS WEEK

Most junior high and middle school kids are searching for their own identity, apart from the family. But their families are still an essential support for them. Sometimes this can be frustrating and can cause tension in a family. This TalkSheet will help your kids understand their family and teach them how to strengthen their family ties.

It's important for you to remember that there are different types of families within society—traditional families, divorced families, single-parent families, or foster families. Don't assume that all your kids live in a traditional two-parent home. Be extra sensitive to those kids who may be feeling the hurt and confusion of divorce and family separation.

OPENER

Everyone has a family of some kind—that's why families are often portrayed on television. Ask your kids to think of as many TV families as they can and keep a list of these on a whiteboard or poster board. What is each family like? Which one would they like to be a member of? Why or why not? How does TV portray family life compared to real life? Is it accurate of families today?

Or get out your Internet surfing skills and find some statistics or facts about families to read to the group. Some of your group may not know what percentage of families are mixed, step-parent families, split families, foster families, and more. For the most recent statistics and information, check out www.childstats.gov or www.fedstats.gov. Read the information or statistics to your group. Are they surprising? Why or why not? What do the statistics say about families today?

THE DISCUSSION, BY THE NUMBERS

1. Ask them to share experiences or stories of their memorable family times. You should hear about some positive experiences that your kids have had with their families.

2. What words did your kids choose to describe their families? To keep this discussion on a positive note, point out that no family is perfect—all families have ups and downs. But sometimes it is easier to remember the hard or bad times rather than the good times. Ask the group to list other descriptive words about their families.

3. Allow them to share the changes they would like to see. You'll most likely get a lot of different responses, so make a list of their suggestions on

the whiteboard or poster board. Then you may want to cross off all those that are unrealistic (such as "get rid of my two sisters" or "sell my baby brother") and with the rest, brainstorm ways they make these changes happen It's good for kids to vent about their home life, but you also need to be supportive of family life. Try to keep a healthy balance. Listen to and talk about the complaints, but don't let this become a bash session against their parents or guardians.

4. What would your kids like to know more about? This can be used as a checklist to generate future topics as well as a discussion topic itself. Spend a few minutes brainstorming ways to learn more information about the topics checked. Is there one or two that your kids want to talk more about?

5. Ask those who share to focus on one verse in particular. If you choose Ephesians 6:1-4, talk about the two-way street in a parent-child relationship. Then discuss what your kids can do to improve the relationships they have at home.

THE CLOSE

No family is perfect because no family members are perfect. But family members can work together and make changes to make things better. Family relationships aren't only their parents' responsibility—it's theirs too. There are many things that kids can do to encourage their family relationships. Are they willing to try?

Communicate your willingness to help those who are having problems at home. You're there to listen to them. Pay close attention to your kids who may show signs of domestic violence or sexual abuse. For information on dealing with abuse, contact Child Help USA (www.childhelpusa.org) or Prevent Child Abuse (www.pcain.org). If you suspect an abusive situation, you are required by law to report it to the authorities.

MORE

- Dare your kids to commit to changing one thing about how they treat their family. Do they need to be more patient? More encouraging? More obedient to their parents? Nicer to their siblings? Encourage them set a realistic goal and then consciously make an effort to change how they act.
- Watch a TV show or a movie involving a family. You can either do this together as a group or individually at home. Ask your group to observe what types of family are shown and note the positive and negative aspects of the family. How realistic is the family? What stereotypes of families are shown through this TV family?

MUSIC TO MY EYES

1. Circle the words below that describe music videos.

exciting	weird	uplifting	non-Christian
boring	funny	depressing	crazy
sexy	scary	sick	helpful
violent	dumb	artistic	surprising
confusing	interesting	dangerous	dishonest

2. How often do you watch music videos?

☐ Every day   ☐ Once or twice a week
☐ Three or four times a week   ☐ Never

3. Name one of your **favorite** music videos. Why do you like it?

4. What do you think of the following statements? Answer **R (right on), S (sometimes)** or **N (no way).**

Music videos don't make much sense to me._____

Music videos don't have anything to do with the song._____

Teenagers don't interpret music videos the same way parents do._____

Music videos are fun to watch._____

There's too much sex and violence in music videos._____

I would like to be in a music video._____

It's better to listen to music than to watch it._____

5. What does God say about music videos? Check out **Colossians 2:8** and write down what you think it says.

MUSIC TO MY EYES [music videos]

THIS WEEK

The changes in music and technology, especially in the past 20 years or so, have changed the ways that youth today view and listen to music. Teenagers today see music videos almost everywhere—on TV stations (like VH1, MTV, CMT), in advertisements, in movies, and on the Internet. Kids can download music video clips from nearly any music Internet homepage.

With all these changing factors, it's important to talk about what videos your kids watch, how they are influenced by them, and how they can make decisions about them in the future.

OPENER

Videotape or rent some music videos. Check out TV stations like MTV, VH1 (pop), or CMT (country). Be sure to preview the entire tape and all videos before you show them to your group. Or videotape some commercials from TV that have music videos in them. Most music TV stations will have them, as well as prime time sitcom stations. Show them to your group. Did they like the video ad or not? What did the music video have to do with the advertisement?

THE DISCUSSION, BY THE NUMBERS

1. Why did they pick the words they did? Ask your kids to explain why they chose them—you'll probably get a variety of answers. Are there more words to describe music videos that aren't on the list?

2. Ask for a show of hands to find out who watches music videos the most and who watches the least. You may find that some don't watch them at all. Then ask them where they watch them the most—on TV? the Internet? On their computers via CD?

3. Ask your kids to give the names of their favorite videos and keep track of them on a whiteboard or poster board. Then ask why they like the videos. Do they like the style of music? Are the graphics catchy? Does the video tell a story? What makes a music video questionable? Point out that your kids are impacted much more by what they see than what they hear.

4. You may want to group the kids together based on their answers. What are their specific reasons for their choices? Ask them to share examples of specific videos that they have in mind. How does listening to the music differ from watching it? What do they like better?

5. Ask for volunteers to share their answers. What does the verse say to them? How do they view music videos in light of this verse?

THE CLOSE

Music videos are seen everywhere and are easily accessible. There's a difference between hearing and seeing the music. How does "seeing" the music change the way they understand the music?

Communicate with your kids that they have choices about what they put in their minds and bodies. Videos aren't necessarily bad, but they often don't reflect Christian values.

It's important to make the best use of time. Time is valuable. Are your students making the best use of the time that God has given them? Do your kids consider watching videos a good use of time?

MORE

● Choose a song that has an accompanying video. In the group, play just the song for your kids to listen to. Ask them to write down what they think about the song. What is going on in the song? What do they think the song is about? What pictures can they see in their head?
Then show them the video. How does watching the video change their interpretation of the song? What was different from what they thought? Was their perception accurate or not? How did "seeing" the music change the song?

● Watch thirty minutes of videos with your group. Then rate them—by stars or a scale of 1-10—according to a list you've put together with them. Do they support or tear down Christian values? What values are being promoted, glamorized or exploited? Is sex, violence, drug use, or negative behaviors shown in the video? Decide what videos rated the highest and why. Which ones didn't rate well?

● There's a fine line between mainstream and Christian musical groups today. Some groups (such as Sixpence None the Richer and Jars of Clay) have crossed over to mainstream. Some mainstream groups write songs that reflect Christian values (sometimes not intentionally) or refer to God. Other groups have Christians in them, regardless of their music.
With this in mind, discuss with your kids what they think classifies a Christian band. What bands do they listen to that are Christian? What do they think about Christians in mainstream bands, or those bands that crossover to mainstream music?

DRINK. DRANK. DRUNK.

1. What do you think? Drinking alcohol—

   ❏ makes me look cool.
   ❏ is okay if done in moderation.
   ❏ is fun.
   ❏ is okay if you're old enough.
   ❏ is sinful.
   ❏ isn't a wise thing to do.

2. Kylie can't stand to be teased anymore. She wouldn't go to a party because she knew the other kids would be drinking. She didn't want to put herself in danger of being tempted to drink too. Now she is being ridiculed for her decision by her friends at school.

   Did Kylie make the right choice by not going to the party?

   What should Kylie do about the teasing?

3. Put a ☆ next to those that you believe are **true**.
   * Alcohol is a drug and should be illegal like other drugs.
   * There's nothing wrong with drinking if you don't get drunk.
   * It should be legal for teenagers to drink wine and beer.
   * Teenagers should try alcohol once, just to see what it's like.
   * People who drink have more fun at parties than people who don't.
   * Alcohol consumption is a personal choice.
   * Drinking is okay for high schoolers, but not for junior highers or middle schoolers.
   * Alcohol can hurt a growing body.
   * Kids my age drink all the time.
   * Underage drinking goes against what the Bible says.

4. You're at a party and one of your friends offers you some soda that you know has been spiked with alcohol. **What** will you do?

5. Does God **approve of** drinking? What **message** do you get from these verses?

   Proverbs 23:29-35

   Isaiah 5:11-12

   1 Corinthians 6:12-13

   Ephesians 5:18

DRINK, DRANK, DRUNK [a l c o h o l]

THIS WEEK

The influence of alcohol is everywhere. Teenagers see it used, talked about, and glamorized on TV, on the radio, and on the Internet. Kids of all ages are consuming alcohol of all kinds, from wine coolers to hard liquor. This TalkSheet gives you a forum to discuss drinking and what a Christian young person should do about alcohol.

OPENER

There are several reasons why teenagers drink alcohol. This intro will give you a feel for what your kids think about drinking. You may want to start by asking your group these questions—Why do people their age drink? Where do they see alcohol advertised the most? Where do teenagers see alcohol drank the most? With a show of hands, how many think that their peers drink at least once a week? At least once a month? How about never?

Keep a list on the whiteboard to refer to later. Be sure to set the tone for the discussion by listening carefully to the opinions of each of the group members. Wait to state your opinion—they'll be more likely listen to you later and respect your thoughts. And remember to encourage them to respect each other's thoughts. This can be a touchy subject, depending on your group, so try extra hard to keep the discussion moving in a positive, yet challenging direction.

THE DISCUSSION, BY THE NUMBERS

1. Your group may have some different opinions. That's good—let your kids debate their answers by giving reasons for their opinions.

2. This tension-getter will help the kids talk about the peer pressure concerning alcohol. Have your group consider different approaches Kylie could use. How would they deal with this situation?

3. You may want to split up the kids into groups based on how they answered the questions. The groups can then debate each of the statements. Focus attention on the consequences of drinking—what it does to friendships, families, parents, and individuals.

4. Your kids may not want to be honest with this one! Peer pressure is the driving force behind drinking and it's very influential. It's important for your kids to think about how they'll respond to the pressures of drinking. Depending on your group, you may want to brainstorm different ways of resisting the pressure and saying no.

5. Now's the time to discuss with your kids God's

view of drinking. They'll want to know if Christ drank wine or why he turned water into wine. Be prepared to give them an answer. Christ most likely did drink wine as a drink, not as a way to abuse alcohol. People abuse alcohol—they use it to ease their loneliness, failure, and depression. There's a huge difference between drinking wine as a beverage and going overboard on alcohol.

THE CLOSE

Young people today associate fun with drinking or doing drugs. It's important to communicate to your group the dangers of drinking—not just the moral implications. Drinking ruins lives, destroys families, and causes thousands of deaths each year. Junior high and middle school kids are especially vulnerable to the addiction of alcohol and drugs. And drinking is extremely dangerous during these growing years.

Challenge your kids to say no to drinking. Communicate that although the Bible talks about drinking wine, its warns not to abuse alcohol (Proverbs 20:1; 23:19-21). If any of your kids are struggling with alcohol, it is imperative that they get help by talking with a trusted adult. They must break the downward spiral now, before its too late.

Saying no to drinking—and any peer pressure—requires self-control. It takes a strong person to stand up for their bodies and minds, but your kids aren't standing alone. Encourage them to ask God for strength and wisdom to say no.

MORE

● Take some time to talk about alcoholism. This is a commonly occurring disease among families—even Christian families—today. Talk about the dangers of alcoholism and how one can tell is someone is an alcoholic. Point out that someone who is drunk has no right to hit or abuse anyone of any age. If any of your kids are facing abusive situations, encourage them to talk with a trusted adult. For more information on alcoholism and other links, visit NIAAA (www.niaaa.nih.gov).

● Have your kids bring in examples of how media portrays drinking. Have them bring in clips of TV shows, advertisements, media clips, songs or other examples of how drinking is shown. Discuss with them how they are being bombarded with pressures to drink and the idea that drinking is okay. How does the media portray drinking? Does it ever deal with the consequences or dangers of it?

WANTING IT ALL

1. If you had **all the money** you wanted, what would you buy?

2. What best describes your current financial (money) situation? **(circle one)**
   a. My family has too much money.
   b. I waste a lot of money.
   c. My family doesn't have enough money.
   d. I wish my family had more money, even though we really don't need anything.
   e. I deserve more allowance than I get.
   f. I'm jealous of others who have more money than I do.

3. Check the following boxes if you've ever—
   ❑ spent money to impress someone.
   ❑ put more food on your plate than you could eat.
   ❑ wished you had something you couldn't afford.
   ❑ thrown away something valuable.

4. Do you **agree (A)** or **disagree (D)** with the following statements?
   ___ Being rich is a blessing from God.
   ___ Getting rich is a good way to enjoy life.
   ___ People have the right to do anything they want with their money.
   ___ People should share what they have with others.
   ___ It's wrong to have more money than you need.
   ___ Everything I have belongs to God.

5. Pick one of the following Bible verses to read, and rewrite in your own words.

   Matthew 6:19-21

   Mark 8:34-36

   1 Samuel 2:7-8

WANTING IT ALL [materialism]

THIS WEEK

Teenagers in the U.S. are saturated by a culture that more than any other values money and possessions. Your kids feel the pressure everywhere they go. Take shopping malls, for example—they've become one of America's most popular hangouts! Teenagers spend more money today than ever on CDs, video games, movies, and clothes. Unfortunately, not much has been done to teach kids about materialism and the dangers of getting caught up in wanting it all. This session will help your youth understand the materialistic world they live in.

OPENER

You may want to start by asking your kids to make a list of all the material things that they or their families own. This means everything—beds, TVs, radios, CDs, video games, et cetera. Make a combined list on a whiteboard or poster board. Some families will have more than one item, like a radio or TV. You may want to illustrate how much stuff Americans have—most of which they don't need to survive! Put a circle around those that are necessary for survival (probably not very many).

Want another idea? Play a version of "The Price is Right" using pictures of expensive items cut out of magazines. If your group is big, split the group up into teams so everyone can play. Then ask each person or team how much they think an item is worth. Whoever guesses the closest can either (you decide) get a point or gain some amount of money. However you want to play is fine, depending on how much time you have. Whatever team ends up with the most points or the most money wins.

THE DISCUSSION, BY THE NUMBERS

1. Make a list of all the things your kids want to buy. When you're done, have them circle the things on the list they think they need, as opposed to the things they want. Communicate with them the difference between needing and wanting—some kids don't understand the difference.

2. Most of your kids might complain about the lack of money. Allow them to share their feelings about their personal money situation. Does money equal power? Why or why not?

3. This item will show your kids that they do have a lot of material possessions. Get them to focus on their feelings. How does it feel to have so much? How does it feel to be envious, jealous, or greedy? How do they think kids in other cultures who have nothing might feel?

4. Hold a vote on each of the statements, according to how your kids answered. If everyone agrees on a particular statement, go to the next one. If there are different opinions on one, ask them to defend their points of view. You may want to display the words Strongly Agree and Strongly Disagree on opposite sides of the room, with Agree and Disagree somewhere in the middle. Have the student move and stand near their vote and debate their reasons.

5. Choose a few of the answers and discuss with them how God feels about money. Point out that money is not evil, but the love of it—greed—is sinful.

THE CLOSE

Materialism is a trap—it's easy to get caught up in wanting it all. Money doesn't buy happiness. The Bible teaches the love of money is idolatry and says "you cannot serve two masters" (Matthew 6:24). Money buys things, but not the things of God—happiness, joy, love, peace—and most importantly, eternal life.

Discuss with the group how Jesus lived and how he challenged his disciples to leave everything and follow him. Although times are different, we're still called to follow him and leave our wants behind. He'll give us what need (and more) if we trust and follow him.

What is one thing that your kids can change about their lifestyle to make them a little less materialistic? Brainstorm with them how to change what they think about possessions. What can they do to make a small change or two?

MORE

- There are many people out there in need of clothes, food, and Christian love. Together with your kids, plan a Christian service project for those who don't have what they need. This can be a big project—possibly traveling to help in another city or foreign country—or something smaller, such as collecting clothing, food, having a garage sale for a charity, or working in a shelter.
- Discuss with the group how they are influenced by the media. What messages about money does the TV, radio, and Internet send? How are they affected by the ads that are everywhere, from billboards to junk mail?
- How do your kids spend their money? Have them keep track of everything that they spend money on in a given week and write it down. Was what they bought something they needed—or wanted? They'll be surprised to see how they've spent their money!

GOD TALK

1. If you could pray for only **three things**, they would be—

2. Is God listening? Which one do you believe to be true about your prayers?
   a. God hears my prayers and answers them.
   b. God hears my prayers, but doesn't always answer them.
   c. God doesn't hear my prayers.

3. **Circle** those that are true for you.
   a. I pray before every meal.
   b. I pray while I'm at school.
   c. I pray for other people.
   d. I praise and thank God in my prayers.
   e. I'm embarrassed to pray in public.
   f. I only pray for myself.

4. Eric's parents were fighting all the time—and he prayed that God would help out. He didn't want them to divorce. But three weeks later, his mom and dad told him they were separating. Eric is mad at God and isn't sure anymore if prayer makes a difference.

   Why do you think God didn't answer his prayer?

   Are Eric's feelings toward God okay?

   What can Eric do to deal with his parents' situation?

   How should Eric approach God now?

5. Match the Bible verse with the correct sentence.
   1. Matthew 6:9-13   a. Prayer can lead to peace.
   2. Luke 5:16   b. Jesus prayed often.
   3. Philippians 4:6-7   c. I should pray for others.
   4. 1 Timothy 2:1-4   d. The Bible tells me how to pray.
   5. 1 John 5:14-16   e. God hears my prayers.

From *Junior High-Middle School TalkSheets—Updated!* by David Lynn. Permission to reproduce this page granted only for use in the buyer's own youth group. www.YouthSpecialties.com

29

GOD TALK [prayer]

THIS WEEK

Prayer is a conversation with God. Some kids don't think they need to pray or don't feel like it. But both talking and listening to God are crucial for understanding God and growing closer to him. This TalkSheet offers your group the opportunity to take a closer look at the importance of prayer.

OPENER

Many young people are intimidated and self-conscious about praying in front of others. Some kids who don't pray a lot may feel guilty when talking about prayer. So to start this one off, have the group write a personal letter to Jesus. Remind them that he is a real person who is waiting to hear from them. Jump start them with ideas for their letter—thanking him for something they have or telling him something that's going on in their life.

They most likely won't want to share these letters. If you think they'd be open to it, ask for volunteers to share bits of their letters. Otherwise explain to them that each of their letters is a prayer. Every time they communicate or talk to God, they're praying! Prayer doesn't have to mean getting down on their knees with their hands folded—prayer can happen anytime, anywhere.

THE DISCUSSION, BY THE NUMBERS

1. Make a list of the things the kids chose and ask why they chose these. Be careful to keep your kids focused on the purpose of prayer. You may want to circle requests that are unrealistic (such as "give me all A's in all my classes"). Remind them that God isn't a genie, granting them their every wish. He does, however, listen to their needs and concerns and will answer their prayers.

2. Ask the kids to give examples or reasons for choosing their statements. Be prepared to talk about how God answers prayers. Some won't understand or believe that God hears their prayers and answers them. Point out that God does answer all prayers—with a yes, a no, or a wait (this can be discussed even more in question 4.)

3. Discuss these statements in a general sense. Should a junior high and middle school student should pray before every meal, pray at school, pray in public, and so on? They can pray without closing their eyes, bowing their heads, or using formal language. Prayer is like a conversation with a friend—in this case, their friend in heaven.

4. This tension-getter gives the group a chance to talk about prayers in a real life situation. Give the kids time to talk about why they think God doesn't answer some prayers like Eric's.

5. What statements did they match with the verses? Ask them to summarize what they've learned about prayer from the Bible verses. You may want to add what you've learned about prayer from the Bible or real life experiences. How has prayer changed you?

THE CLOSE

As you close, keep the following points in mind—

* It's hard to have a relationship with God without talking to him—just as it's hard to keep a friendship without talking.
* Prayer isn't magic—it's a conversation with God. He wants us to talk with him, using our own language and letting him know what's on our minds.
* Instead of challenging the kids to do something unrealistic—such as praying for an hour each day—encourage them to begin with two minutes of prayer a day. If they are already praying two, have them strive for four. Challenge them with manageable goals.
* Also, remind them that prayer involves listening, too. Let them know that sometimes it's good to just sit back, relax in a quiet place, and reflect on what's going on in their lives and what God would wants them to do. God doesn't shout out answers, but he does speak to us through our feelings and thoughts.

Challenge your kids to pray with a pen and paper—to write down things that they are praying for. Have them journal their prayers for a week, then take a look back to see if and how the prayers have been answered. They might have to wait longer than a week. But encourage them to do this. It's a great way to look back and thank God for what he's done!

MORE

* With your group, make a prayer request list and encourage them to pray from the list each day. Use this to illustrate the importance of praying for and supporting each other. Encourage your kids to e-mail you with concerns and prayer requests. Then distribute the list weekly to encourage prayer among the group. Use snail-mail for kids without e-mail. Include praises in this list, too!
* God's model for prayer is the Lord's Prayer. Break your kids up into small groups and give them each a phrase of the prayer to write in their own words. Then together as a group, put all the pieces together and write a group interpretation of the Lord's Prayer.

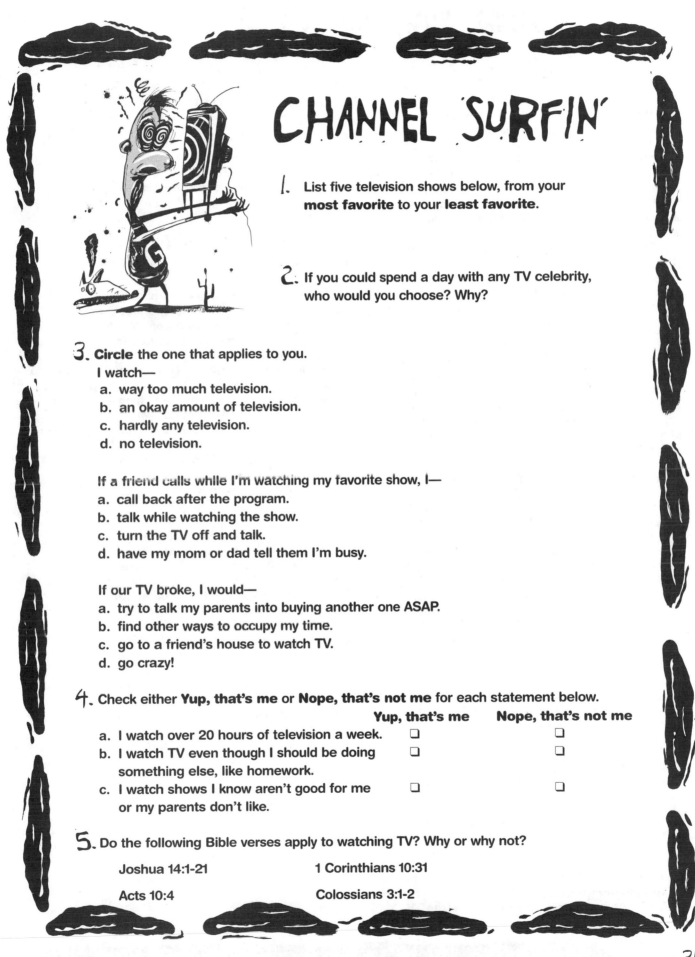

CHANNEL SURFIN'

1. List five television shows below, from your **most favorite** to your **least favorite**.

2. If you could spend a day with any TV celebrity, who would you choose? Why?

3. **Circle** the one that applies to you.
   I watch—
   a. way too much television.
   b. an okay amount of television.
   c. hardly any television.
   d. no television.

   If a friend calls while I'm watching my favorite show, I—
   a. call back after the program.
   b. talk while watching the show.
   c. turn the TV off and talk.
   d. have my mom or dad tell them I'm busy.

   If our TV broke, I would—
   a. try to talk my parents into buying another one ASAP.
   b. find other ways to occupy my time.
   c. go to a friend's house to watch TV.
   d. go crazy!

4. Check either **Yup, that's me** or **Nope, that's not me** for each statement below.

	Yup, that's me	Nope, that's not me
a. I watch over 20 hours of television a week.	❏	❏
b. I watch TV even though I should be doing something else, like homework.	❏	❏
c. I watch shows I know aren't good for me or my parents don't like.	❏	❏

5. Do the following Bible verses apply to watching TV? Why or why not?

   Joshua 14:1-21   1 Corinthians 10:31

   Acts 10:4   Colossians 3:1-2

CHANNEL SURFIN' [television]

THIS WEEK

Television, the tube, the telly (to use British slang), the TV. Call it what you will, but the TV rules the American household. The average person watches hours of television every week. Now, with cable there's a channel for nearly everyone with any interest—from sports lovers to rap music fans. The TV is the life of U.S. popular culture—telling people what they need or don't need, what they should eat, drink, or where, and how they should look, act, and behave.

This TalkSheet raises important questions for Christians. You can't tell your kids to turn the TV off altogether, but you can teach them good viewing skills. The purpose of this session is to talk about TV and teach them how to evaluate what they watch.

OPENER

On a large piece of newsprint or whiteboard, draw a blank television schedule for the week, writing only the days, certain channels, and certain evening times (such as Fox Network, Monday, 7:00 p.m. or NBC, Tuesday, 8:00 p.m.). Then ask the kids to guess or tell you what shows air at those specific times. You'll be surprised how much they know! Have the correct answers available in order to check their responses. For information on show times in your area check out Gist TV (www.gist.com/tv/) or www.askjeeves.com, then type in the keywords, "television shows."

Want to take it further? Ask your group to rank the shows as good, bad, or questionable on a scale of 1-10, with stars, or however you want to. Talk about the different kinds of shows and what age groups they think each show is meant for. Then, discuss how each show portrays people of different ages—especially teenagers, parents, and religion.

THE DISCUSSION, BY THE NUMBERS

1. Your group will have a variety of favorite shows. What do they like about them and why did they chose one over another?

2. Ask the group to share their favorite television personalities and why they'd want to spend a day with that person. What do they like about this person and why?

3. What are the TV watching habits of your group? You'll find that most of their evenings revolve around the TV—even if there's nothing really good on.

4. This activity allows your kids to evaluate their viewing habits. Challenge them to evaluate their TV watching habits and discuss how the TV impacts their lives. Listen to them carefully and save your opinions until the end, if necessary.

5. Ask the kids to share the verses that apply to TV and ask how they apply. Discuss with them how TV be used to glorify God? How do they think Christians should view certain shows? What Christian influences or values to they see in certain programs, if any?

THE CLOSE

TV is entertainment. Billions of dollars are spend on programming every week. But most of what's on TV isn't real—the shows offer an escape from reality. Some youth don't understand that they're watching fiction—shows with beautiful (sometimes perfect) people, numerous special effects, and unrealistic plots.

Brainstorm and make a list of the values that Christians should look for in TV shows. What should Christians keep in mind when watching TV? How do they think saturating their minds with TV shows affects the way they act, talk, and live? How do they think advertisements affect them and what can they do about that as Christians? Challenge them to limit their TV watching and brainstorm other activities they can do to fill the time.

MORE

● What and when are they watching? Ask your kids to keep journal of their weekly TV watching and then bring it in for discussion. Discuss the shows they watched and the amount of time spend watching it compared to the other stuff they did, such as homework, playing sports, eating, talking on the phone, and sleeping.

● And while they're watching the shows, have them pay close attention to the advertisements. What was the ad was telling them? Make a list of all their favorite ads and why the ad appealed to them. Explain that the average 1/2 hour TV show has more than 10 minutes of advertisements—how does that affect the way people think about and spend money?

PEOPLE PLEASER

1. When someone pressures me to do something that
I know is wrong, I—
- ❏ lie and make up an excuse.
- ❏ tell the person I won't do it because it is wrong.
- ❏ just say no.
- ❏ suggest another activity.
- ❏ other—

2. Which is more true? When I'm with my friends—
- ❏ I usually get them to do what I want to do.
- ❏ they usually get me to do what they want to do.

3. Parents or friends? Who would you go to for advice on—

	Parents	Friends
what to wear to school	❏	❏
what kind of music to listen to	❏	❏
what to believe about God	❏	❏
what movie to see	❏	❏
what classes to take	❏	❏
what to do after school	❏	❏

4. Mark each answer with **+ plus sign (yes), – negative sign (no)** or
? question mark (maybe).

___ When someone dares me to do something, I'll do it (rather than be called a wimp).
___ I feel pressured to do things that others are doing, to be accepted.
___ I don't like it when people are mad at me.
___ I try hard to please others.
___ My parents approve of the friends I have.
___ I would do almost anything to have friends.

5. Read the three Bible verses below and match each one with the correct letter
(there are three extra choices).

___ Proverbs 4:13-14
___ Romans 12:1-2
___ 1 Corinthians 15:33

a. Don't conform to the world's pressures.
b. Do whatever feels good.
c. Bad company corrupts (ruins) good character.
d. Be all things to all people.
e. He who has lots of friends will be rich.
f. Hold on to instruction.

PEOPLE PLEASER [peer pressure]

THIS WEEK

Let's face it—peer pressure surrounds teenagers. They spend less time with families, attend classes with large groups of peers, work at jobs with people their age, play sports with friends, and talk on the phone with them. Teenagers learn from, grow with, and are influenced by others their age. This TalkSheet will help you to deal with the real issues facing your kids and the discuss the influences of peer pressure.

OPENER

Announce you're going to conduct a taste test, like those they've seen on TV. Have them taste two different brands of soda (like Coke and Pepsi) or ice cream (or whatever else you'd like), to determine which is best, brand A or brand B.

Beforehand, tell some of your kids to choose brand A. Their job is to persuade the others to pick the same brand. You'll find that some in the group will give in to this pressure and will choose brand A. Keep a tally of the results and then discuss the results. How were the kids influenced by others? Why did they listen to their peers?

Some kids won't be persuaded—congratulate them for having resisted. What made them stick up for their choice? How did they feel when the others were pressuring them? What other feelings or ideas did they have?

DISCUSSION, BY THE NUMBERS

1. Use a few of the specific responses to these situations for discussion. What issues are they dealing with? What are some circumstances they face? How would they respond to a given pressure? Brainstorm some ways to resist peer pressure.

2. Junior high and middle school kids are in the middle—moving away from the parental influence and toward peer pressure. Their peers are becoming a powerful influence. This activity allows you to discuss the pressures they face. To keep the discussion moving, don't ask each one to share individually. Instead, discuss each statement in terms of the average teenager. You might ask, "Who won on these items? Your parents or your friends?" (Keep track of how many picked Parents or Friends.)

3. and 4. Come at these issues from a general perspective. Each one deals with a specific aspect of peer pressure. Phrase your questions so they are giving opinions—not revealing themselves: "What are some things you could do, if your friends called you wimp?" Ask them to think through the consequences of peer pressure by asking, "And then what?" Get them to think about the results of their actions.

5. Some of these statements are wrong. Did they get the correct ones? Look up the verses and match them to the correct phrases, then discuss each one. 1 Corinthians 15:33 is a particularly helpful one for them to keep in mind (and possibly memorize).

THE CLOSE

Based on the response to question 3, you may want to talk about how much your group thinks peer pressure influences them. What's the difference between being self-controlled (a fruit of the Spirit) and other-controlled.

There's nothing wrong with going along with friends—as long as it isn't illegal, unethical, harmful, or likewise. God has given us beliefs and a conscience. He trusts people to make wise choices. Real friends respect each other's opinions and beliefs. If friends can't and won't do that—think about finding some friends that respect you for who you are.

Parents have lived through the teenage years and understand pressures, too! Most adults still deal with peer pressure on certain levels. Encourage your kids to ask their parents questions about how to deal with pressure.

MORE

● Ask your group to find examples in the media of how kids influence other kids. They'll find examples of this pressure (anything from stealing to having sex) on nearly every teenage TV show and in magazine advertisements. Have them bring a few examples of this pressure and discuss if the media portrays peer pressure as good or bad.

● Have your kids make a list of their beliefs and values—then sign the list as a contract for themselves as things they won't compromise on (such as doing drugs or having premarital sex). Encourage them to set personal goals for themselves and to include God in this goal. No temptation is too great to resist with God on their side.

SO NOBODY'S PERFECT

1. What do you think are common sins of people your age?

2. What do you think?

	Definitely	Sometimes	Nope
a. If I sin, God will punish me.	❑	❑	❑
b. When I sin, I feel guilty.	❑	❑	❑
c. I can't stop sinning.	❑	❑	❑
d. I enjoy seeing how much I can get away with.	❑	❑	❑
e. I enjoy doing things I know I shouldn't do.	❑	❑	❑
f. If I knew I could do something wrong without getting caught, I would do it.	❑	❑	❑

3. **True** or **False**—
   a. Some sins are worse than others._____
   b. Christians don't sin on purpose._____
   c. If a sin isn't harmful to anyone, then it's not really a sin._____
   d. If you sin accidentally, then it's not really a sin._____
   e. If you ask God to forgive your sins, then it's okay to sin again._____

4. Check out **Romans 3:23**—what does it say in your own words?

SO NOBODY'S PERFECT [s i n]

THIS WEEK

What is sin? It can be a hard concept for some teenagers to understand, especially when they aren't familiar with the Bible. Society today teaches ideas about sin that are contrary to God's word and argues that there's no such thing as a sin, some sins really aren't sins, or teaching about sin just makes people feel guilty. This TalkSheet will help explain what sin is and open a discussion about sin and what Christians can do about it.

OPENER

Since it's hard for some to understand sin (besides doing something wrong), ask your group to answer the following questions—

• What does sin look like (in your imagination)?
• How would you describe sin?
• What causes you to sin?
• How much sin is too much?

They'll probably have a bunch of different answers. Take some time to make a master list of these answers. Why did they pick the answers they did? What helps them understand sin better?

Or collect and pass out newspapers or magazines to the kids and ask them to find a few examples of sin. Go around and have them share one or two examples that they found. What was the sin? Why is it considered a sin? How would the sin rate on a scale of 1-10?

THE DISCUSSION, BY THE NUMBERS

1. Make a list of all the sins they wrote down. Ask the kids to circle which ones they think are the worst and what sins they think are the most common. After some discussion, challenge them to reach a definition of what sin is.

2. Approach this discussion with general statements—not personal. Don't force your kids to reveal their individual answers. Ask the question with something like, "Do you believe God punishes people for sinning? If so, how?"

3. As your kids share their answers, encourage them to think of biblical support for their opinions. It'll take some time for them to find some verses, but that's okay. You may want to focus on the last statement and talk about this—many junior high and middle schoolers don't understand repentance. You may have to explain that it means being truly sorry for their sin and being willing to change.

4. These verses focus on God's grace and forgiveness. Some of your kids won't understand the concept of grace, so be prepared to explain this and give examples. You may want to discuss 1 John 1:9 and have some of them share their paraphrases.

THE CLOSE

Everyone—parents, pastors, teachers, and friends—sins. It's a fact. They are all human and they all fall short of the glory of God. The good news is that although sin distances us from God, it never separates us completely from his love. God is faithful and forgives us our sins (1 John 1:9). They get a fresh start whenever they ask for God's forgiveness.

Are there one or two sins that each group member is struggling with or feeling guilty about? You may want to ask group members to write down their sins on a piece of paper. Then demonstrate God's refining fire—his forgiveness—by burning the papers in a fire outside (just be careful!). Or (the safer option) have your kids rip them into tiny pieces. Either activity shows what Christ does with our sins—forgives and forgets. You may want to give them a moment of silent prayer or reflection time. And remind them that they need to forgive themselves too.

MORE

● The Bible is chock full of examples of God's grace and forgiveness. There are several examples in the miracles and life of Christ, who showed love and mercy to sinners. In fact, Jesus hung out with unclean sinners (like Mary, a former prostitute). Have the group find some of these examples and list them on a whiteboard or poster board.

● Discuss with your group the importance of forgiving others like God forgives them. What makes it hard to forgive and forget with your friends or family? What sins are easier to forgive than others? How can they deal with these sins and get over the hurt caused by others? Challenge your kids to confront and forgive one person this week.

DO-SOMETHING @WORLD.NET

1. Can you list **everything** that's in your bedroom (even down to the last shirt)? Try it and see what you come up with (use the back of this paper if you need more room).

2. How would you complete the following sentence? When I see someone who is really poor—

   - ❑ I feel pity for them.
   - ❑ I look the other way.
   - ❑ I try to give them something.
   - ❑ I get angry.
   - ❑ I don't care.
   - ❑ I feel guilty.
   - ❑ I do whatever I can to help them.
   - ❑ I feel frustrated.

3. If you had to be **one** of the following, which would it be?
   - ❑ Homeless
   - ❑ Physically disabled
   - ❑ Mentally handicapped
   - ❑ Hungry and unable to obtain food
   - ❑ Old and living in a rest home
   - ❑ Sick and unable to afford medical care

4. What do you think? **Y (yes)** or **N (no)**—
   ___ a. One person cannot make a difference in the world.
   ___ b. It's God's will for some people to be poor.
   ___ c. Christians should be concentrating on solving the problems of the world.
   ___ d. The care of the underprivileged in this country is the responsibility of the government.
   ___ e. If people are poor, it's their own fault.
   ___ f. If I could help someone who is poor, sick, or hungry, I would.

5. Pick one of the following Bible verses to **read and rewrite** in your own words.

   Proverbs 14:31   Isaiah 3:13-15

   Proverbs 21:13

DO-SOMETHING@WORLD.NET [Christian social action]

THIS WEEK

There's an overwhelming number of problems in the world—everything from poverty to social injustice. Junior high and middle school kids are able to give a lot, but many don't get encouraged to get into action. This TalkSheet allows you to discuss how your kids can make a difference in the world by helping others who are less fortunate.

OPENER

Are your kids up-to-date with what's going on in the world? You may want to distribute newspapers and news magazines (such as *TIME* and *Newsweek*) and have groups find as many stories as possible about needy people and world problems. Allow five to 10 minutes for the search. Then have them share the stories. It may be helpful to have a world map there for them to see where the problem is going on. You may want to put stickers or marks on the places where the problems are taking place—both international or in the U.S.

What are the needs of others in the world? Role-play and discuss some situations of those in need—having no fresh water, eating only rice once every-other day, battling a disease without funds to get money, not being able to worship freely, etc. How would your kids feel in these situations? How would their priorities be different? Would these situations change their understanding of God?

THE DISCUSSION, BY THE NUMBERS

1. Most of your kids could fill an entire page with their answers. Most youth in the U.S. have more than they think. In fact, kids their age in other countries would not believe how much teenagers in the U.S. have.

2. Ask for volunteers to share how they completed this sentence. Ask them to find examples of how Christ responded to someone who was very poor. Discuss how he treated them.

3. As they share, encourage the kids to talk about their answers as if they were really in that condition. How does it feel? What choices do they have? What will they do? Who will they turn to for help?

4. These statements deal with how things can and should be changed. Teenagers need to know they can make a difference, in spite of the overwhelming nature of the world's problems. Spend extra time on the last statement. Ask them for ideas to help someone less fortunate than themselves.

5. They know that God loves helping others—look at what Jesus did! What do these verses say to your group? Ask them to state one thing they've learned from the passages.

THE CLOSE

God has given everyone gifts and abilities—big and small—to help those in need. He can use each person in the room to make a difference in the world. Look at Mark 6:39-55 for example—he fed five thousand people from one small lunch! In the same way, God can and will take whatever they have to offer him and bless it. Because God sees and knows all things, even our somewhat small efforts will play a big role.

MORE

● Prayer is one way that your kids can help those in need. You may want to make a list of all the problems that were discussed in the introduction. Then pass this list out and ask your kids to pray for one world problem each day. Encourage them to keep an eye out for world news and keep it in their prayers. For the latest world news, check out www.cnn.com or www.nbc.com.

● As a group, sponsor a needy child through an Christian organization. There are several organizations, including World Vision (www.wvi.org) or Compassion International (www.ci.org). By doing small fundraisers or pooling their money, your group will be able to help a child in need and experience first-hand how to support someone in need.

● Dare your kids to get out there and do something! With your group, plan a service project or outreach to help those in need. A useful resource for planning is the *Ideas Library: Camps, Retreats, Missions & Service Ideas* (Youth Specialties).

WHAT'S IT ALL ABOUT?

1. Meesha goes to church almost every Sunday with her parents. She doesn't always understand the sermons, but she likes the singing. She doesn't attend the youth group meetings. At school, she's a good student and doesn't give anyone any trouble. She has lots of friends.

   Do you think Meesha is a Christian?

2. Check the following that are necessary for being a Christian.

   ❑ Be baptized.
   ❑ Be confirmed.
   ❑ Ask Jesus into your heart.
   ❑ Believe the Bible is true.
   ❑ Be a church member.
   ❑ Stop committing sins.
   ❑ Be born again.

   ❑ Belong to the right kind of church.
   ❑ Repent of your sins.
   ❑ Love God and love others.
   ❑ Act like a Christian.
   ❑ Give money to the church.
   ❑ Read the Bible and pray every day.
   ❑ Join the church choir.

3. What's the best reason to become a Christian? **Circle one**.

   To go to heaven.

   To have a better life on earth.

   To experience the love of God in my life.

   To get everything I want.

4. One thing I don't understand about the **Christian faith** is—

5. Match the following Bible verses with the words in the right-hand column.

   1. Matthew 6:33
   2. Matthew 16:24
   3. Matthew 22:37
   4. Matthew 22:39
   5. Romans 12:1-2
   6. 1 Corinthians 10:31

   a. Love others
   b. Follow Christ
   c. Glorify God
   d. Love God
   e. Seek God's kingdom
   f. Do God's will

WHAT'S IT ALL ABOUT? [basic Christianity]

THIS WEEK

This TalkSheet is designed to help explore some of the basic ideas about Christianity. Some of your kids will be on different levels—you may have to add ideas or questions based on your group. You may also want to emphasize specific beliefs or doctrines within the context of this TalkSheet.

Make sure that you do your homework for this discussion. Be prepared for those student who won't understand Christian concepts such as "born again", "be confirmed", or "ask Jesus in your heart". Don't assume that your kids will understand all these! You'll probably have to explain a few or all of these.

OPENER

Are your kids listening? How much do they know? Check it out by asking an adult member of your church, a youth sponsor, or your senior pastor to prepare a five-minute message. It should contain some subtle half-truths that aren't biblically correct. You may want to prep your kids before hand—maybe have them write down any ideas they disagree with. Then see if they picked up any questionable ideas from the sermon.

Or play Bible Trivia—you may be surprised what they do or don't know! You can either pick out some questions before hand or check out www.Biblequizzes.com or www.bible-trivia.com. Split the group up into teams and take turns asking questions. The team with the most points wins the game.

THE DISCUSSION, BY THE NUMBERS

1. This tension-getter was designed to help your kids think about what it means to be a Christian. You might add more information about Meesha, a little at a time. Mention some extra facts—she was baptized as an infant, she doubts the Bible is the Word of God, she went forward to receive Christ at a youth conference, she sometimes swears, she has started smoking cigarettes, and so on. The main point is that it's not easy to know whether not people are genuinely Christians or not.

2. What statements on this list are necessary in order to be a Christian? Discuss each of these—you may want to have some verses to help the discussion. Focus on what the cores of Christian beliefs are and which ones are most important

3. Communicate that the Christian faith requires a relationship with God. You may want or need to read some verses or explain the death and resurrection of Christ. Again, don't assume that your

kids understand everything about being a Christian. Encourage them to ask questions and remind them that you'll be there to talk with them one-on-one later.

4. Now's the time to try to clear up any misunderstandings that the kids might have about the Christian life. Before you take over answering, encourage them to share their views and understandings with each other.

5. After the kids have completed matching up the verses with the statements, choose one or two to discuss with them. Ask them if they have questions or any ideas about what the verses say about Christians.

THE CLOSE

Explain, encourage, and invite! You may have kids who need some one-on-one answers about being a Christian. This is an open door for presenting the gospel and salvation through Jesus. Assure them that no question is stupid—they don't have to understand everything about the Christian faith! The Christian life is a journey.

Encourage your kids to grow in the Christian faith, to get reading their Bibles and in conversation with God through prayer. As a Christian, they have a gift to give—the message of God's love and salvation. If they want to understand Christianity better, they need to get to know God better. Encourage them and provide them with ways to learn more about the faith. Recommend a devotional or Bible reading program, organize a small group Bible study— you need to jumpstart them and encourage their walk with God.

MORE

- Do your kids know what a creed is? Do they have their own personal creed—a statement of their personal beliefs? Have them write one. Encourage them to put it in a visible place and read it when they start to doubt their beliefs or when people question what they believe and why.
- Or have each of your youth write a letter stating their spiritual goals and how they want to grow as Christians. Give them envelopes, which they will address to themselves and seal. Mail the letters to them anywhere from six months to a year.
- You may want to have your kids do some research on the Internet for information on Christian doctrines—sanctification, conversion, grace, justification, or creation. Some of these can be pretty heavy subjects—be sure not to overload them! You may want to make this a group effort and work with each other.

WISE UP

1. **Who would you go to for advice if you had to make an important decision?**

   mother   youth pastor   coach

   best friend   teacher   my dog

   pastor   school counselor   fortune teller

   grandparent   boyfriend   nobody

   father   girlfriend   Internet

2. **Check the areas where you need to have more wisdom.**
   - ❏ My schoolwork
   - ❏ My friendships
   - ❏ My family life
   - ❏ My use of money
   - ❏ My feelings
   - ❏ My ability to listen to advice
   - ❏ My time
   - ❏ Other—

3. **What three things listed below would help you become a wiser person?**

   a. Reading more books

   b. Taking more risks

   c. Praying more often

   d. Watching more television

   e. Choosing wiser friends

   f. Asking more questions

   g. Thinking before I act

   h. Going with my feelings

   i. Studying the Bible more often

   j. Asking God for more wisdom

4. **What if you read this e-mail?**

   Dear junior high or middle school student,

   I'm a mother of three kids-two teenage daughters and one teenage son. Here's my problem-none of them will listen to my advice. They (especially the oldest, my son) think they know it all. I love them and am concerned for their future and want to give them some of my wisdom. I don't want them to make the same mistakes I made or those I've seen others make. What can I do?

   -At The End of My Rope

   What advice would you give this mother?

5. **The following verses talk about wisdom. Check out each verse and match it with the correct statement.**

   1. Proverbs 1:8: It's wise to—
   2. Proverbs 3:5-6: It's wise to—
   3. Proverbs 4:23: It's wise to—
   4. Proverbs 10:19-20: It's wise to—
   5. Proverbs 12:22: It's wise to—
   6. Proverbs 22:24-25: It's wise to—
   7. Proverbs 29:11: It's wise to—

   a. control what you say

   b. trust in God wholeheartedly

   c. listen to your parents

   d. guard your heart

   e. control you temper

   f. speak the truth

   g. choose friends carefully

WISE UP [w i s d o m]

THIS WEEK

Kids hear advice from friends, teachers, parents, and the media—just to name a few sources. Who do they listen to? What will they believe? How are they able to sort out all these ideas and information? This TalkSheet is created to discuss the need for guidance and ends with a discussion on God's Word as the ultimate source of wisdom.

OPENER

Before this activity, you'll need something to write on (a newsprint, poster board, or white board), something to write with, and a few other items—horoscopes, some large dice, a deck of cards, a Magic 8-ball, "cootie-catcher" (ask a junior high girl), advice column clips (check a newspaper or teen magazine), a Bible, and so on. Start by asking your kids to name the problems they face daily and list them on the whiteboard or poster board. (For example, what to eat for breakfast, what to wear, who to eat lunch with, or how to study for a test). Then split your group into smaller groups and give each a few of the problems listed. Their mission is to solve or answer these problems by using a "tool of wisdom"—one of the "other items" you brought with you—as their only way to make a decision or figure out their dilemmas. Then debrief the group on these sources of wisdom and how helpful (or unhelpful) they are.

THE DISCUSSION, BY THE NUMBERS

1. As the group shares their answers, make a list and find out who your group considers the best advice-giver. Why did they pick who they did? What was the most popular choice? Who do they consider to be most trustworthy?

2. Let the kids share the different areas where they need to have more wisdom. You may want to start the discussion by sharing a experience or story from when you were their age.

3. Compare how this question was answered and talk over each item one at a time. Discuss and encourage those that are positive wisdom builders (a,c,e,f,g,i) and ask why the others aren't such good ways to become wise.

4. This letter from a mother deals with a common problem of parents of teenagers—the know-it-all son or daughter. After the kids share their advice, ask them to think about their own parents' point of view. Are they willing to listen to their parents? Why or why not?

5. The focus here is using the Bible as a source of wisdom for guidance and help. You may want to include a few verses that deal with the future and God being in control. The Proverbs are filled with great tips for being wise and living life.

THE CLOSE

Discuss with your kids how to seek God's wisdom through prayer, Bible study, and the advice from other Christians. Caution the group to be aware of the advice that they get from their friends, the media, and other outside sources—it's easy to hear the wrong message and make the wrong choices. God has given them the ability to discern and evaluate what is going on. And, remind them that "the fear of the Lord is the beginning of knowledge" (Proverbs 1:7)—true wisdom comes from God. The more they love God and keep his commandments, the more wisdom they'll receive.

MORE

● With the group, write down five issues that young people want advice on—choosing friends, dating, dealing with anger, doing drugs, and so on. You may want to have them look for Bible verses that deal with these issues. It may be helpful to use a topical Bible or search an on-line Bible for passages. Have them look through Proverbs as well—Solomon was a smart guy. Then discuss these verses and how they apply. What does God have to say about this?

● Q & A time—you may want to use a panel of adult parents or a combination of adults and kids. Have your kids write questions that they want advice on (make sure these aren't signed). Put these in a box and read them one at a time. Then, have the adults give their advice or opinion on the situation. This is a great way for kids to interact with adults and hear perspectives from other people, not just you or their peers.

● Where do people look for advice in today's society? A few examples include advice columns in newspapers and magazines (such as "Dear Abby"), question and answer columns in teen magazines (such as *Teen* or *Seventeen*), radio or TV shows such as Dr. Laura or Oprah, and self-help books. Which of these have your kids gone to for advice? Why or why not? Take some time to talk about these trends in a society that is seeking wisdom.

ONE IS THE LONELIEST NUMBER

1. **Circle** the following words that describe loneliness.

   depression   time with God   quietness
   rejection   happiness   fright
   hurt   peace   fun
   boredom   sadness   enjoyment

2. Which statement do you think is the most **true**?
   - ❑ Being alone is the same as being lonely.
   - ❑ Being bored is the same as being lonely.

3. Would you **agree** or **disagree** with the statements below?
   a. Everyone is lonely at times.
   b. If you're with other people, you won't be lonely.
   c. If you feel lonely, it's your own fault.
   d. Jesus felt lonely.

4. Who do you think are the most lonely people? Rank the following from **most lonely (1)** to **least lonely (6)**.
   _____ Widows and widowers
   _____ Famous people
   _____ Divorced people
   _____ Young people
   _____ Old people
   _____ Christians

5. Take a look at **1 Kings 19:9-18**. If you were to write a comforting note to Elijah, what would you say?

ONE IS THE LONELIEST NUMBER [l o n e l i n e s s]

THIS WEEK

Young people hear that the teenage years are the best years of their lives. But these years can be very lonely, even in the midst of the carefree fun. This TalkSheet offers your group the chance to talk about their lonely feelings, the causes and cures of loneliness, and how God can help.

OPENER

Before this session, you may want to ask your kids to find examples or stories of loneliness—song lyrics, video clips, poems, stories from a magazine or book, et cetera. Then read, play, or show these examples in the group. What message does each one give about loneliness? What words or characteristics about loneliness come to mind from each example? How is the author or artist feeling and why? How did he or she get over the loneliness, if at all? You may want to make a master list of these characteristics to refer to later.

THE DISCUSSION, BY THE NUMBERS

1. Ask the kids to share and explain their choices. Ask if any other words came to mind and add these to a list of all the words.

2. Young people often assume that if they're bored or alone, then they're lonely. They need to understand they don't always have to be entertained or be with a crowd. In fact, they can be entertained or with their friends and still feel lonely.

3. Focus on b and talk about being alone and being lonely. A person can be alone and not be lonely. Also, focus on the fact that Christ felt rejected, and nothing feels as lonely as being rejected. (See Matthew 13:53-57; Mark 14:27, 31, 50; and Luke 4:24-30.) Kids today think that they must be constantly entertained. In a visual, materialistic culture, they're overloaded and don't know how to deal with being alone. Communicate with them that everyone is differently—some people handle being alone different than others. Remind them that everyone—even teachers, parents, and you—feel lonely sometimes. These alone times aren't bad—they can be healthy. Learning to be content in any circumstance is a sign of real maturity.

4. How is loneliness healthy for some people? Have them share their choices and explain why they ranked them in the order they chose.

5. After they have had some time to write their notes, have the kids read them aloud. Have they ever felt like Elijah? What are some practical solutions to loneliness? There are lots of ways to do this—calling a friend, reading a magazine, trying a new activity, spending time with God (God talk!) What else do your kids suggest?

THE CLOSE

God created us to be in close relationships with other people. We were created to live in families and in community with others. That's why it's important for us to build friendships and protect our relationships.

Christ experienced loneliness. You may want to read a few verses that show Christ being alone. He understands their every emotion and every need. Your kids may feel lonely, but they aren't ever alone. Who can they turn to when they feel down? Encourage them to find one person who they know will encourage them—including you, their teacher, school counselor, or other adult.

MORE

● How do they handle alone time? Challenge your kids to spend a half hour of their time alone, away from everyone—no TV, Internet, radio, or any other distraction. Have them concentrate on being alone with themselves, just sitting, thinking, or praying. What was hard about being alone? What did they do to keep themselves occupied?

● You may want to take time and talk about loneliness versus depression. There is an alarming rate of depression among Americans, including young people. Some of your kids may deal with depression—either their own or a relative's. Loneliness and depression are not the same thing. Make sure that your kids know the difference between being lonely and being depressed. Constant loneliness leads to depression, depression leads to withdrawal and further loneliness. Depression, although it varies person to person, is a chronic, emotional disorder with symptoms of mood swings and suicidal thoughts. For more information and links, check out www.depression.com or www.depression.about.com/health/depression/.

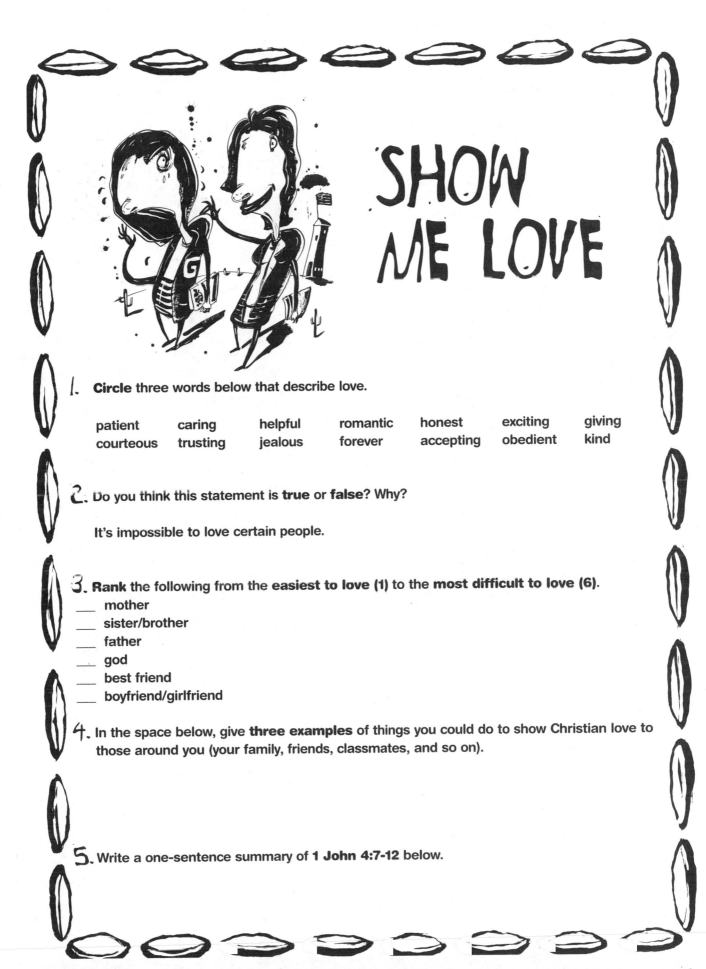

SHOW ME LOVE

1. **Circle** three words below that describe love.

   patient   caring   helpful   romantic   honest   exciting   giving
   courteous trusting jealous   forever   accepting obedient   kind

2. Do you think this statement is **true** or **false**? Why?

   It's impossible to love certain people.

3. **Rank** the following from the **easiest to love (1)** to the **most difficult to love (6)**.
   ___ mother
   ___ sister/brother
   ___ father
   ___ god
   ___ best friend
   ___ boyfriend/girlfriend

4. In the space below, give **three examples** of things you could do to show Christian love to those around you (your family, friends, classmates, and so on).

5. Write a one-sentence summary of **1 John 4:7-12** below.

SHOW ME LOVE [Christian love]

THIS WEEK

There are different ideas about love among teens. Some think it's a kind of gushy, sentimental emotion you have toward someone. Others think it's a physical act, as implied or shown on TV and in movies. A few have heard that it's an action, not an emotion. Our culture and media is saturated with different ideas of love, many of which are untrue and unhealthy. This TalkSheet will help you find out what your kids think about love. It teaches what love is and explains practical ways that your youth can put love into action.

OPENER

Romantic love is the hot issue in all kinds of music—from rap to country ballads. Begin this session by listening to a popular song or by watching a music video that deals with love.

Or start by writing the word love on a large sheet of poster board or whiteboard. Then have your kids list words that describe love—what they think love is and how the media portrays love. You can use this list later to wrap things up.

THE DISCUSSION, BY THE NUMBERS

1. Have the kids share their choices and explain why they chose them. Circle the two that they think are most important.

2. Young people often believe you can only love someone if there is something lovable about him or her. Christian—or agape—love says that they don't look for a lovable quality, but they love in spite of unlovable characteristics. Talk about this concept of love with your group.

3. What reasons do your kids have for their answers? What is hard to love about a person? Why is it hard to love them?

4. Go through the list to see which ones they chose as an example of Christian love. Discuss those that everyone didn't agree on. Brainstorm additional examples of love and talk about the practical ways to demonstrate Christian love.

5. Ask your kids to share what they learned from reading this passage. Focus on the idea that they love others because God loves us. God gives us love so that they can love others as he loves us.

THE CLOSE

As you wrap up, be sure to point out to your kids that love is not a feeling or an emotion, but is a decision they make. The Bible doesn't ask them to like their neighbors—it commands them to love them, even if they're people they don't like.

Challenge your kids to look at people the way Christ did. Every person is a child of God, created in the image of God, and who Christ died for. Today's culture teaches people to use people and love material things—Christ teaches them to simply love others.

Close up by reflecting on the initial list of words that describe love. Discuss how the world portrays love and how Christianity portrays love. What major differences are there? How have people messed up the meaning of love? What would God have to say to our society about love?

MORE

● Ask your kids to think of one person that they have a hard time loving. You may want to point out that a good way to show love to them is to pray for them. Prayer strengthens relationships—and makes them right with God. Encourage your group to do something for that person during the week—pray for them, go out of their way to say hello, or send that person and e-mail or anonymous note. What was hard about showing love to that person? How did their perspective toward that person change?

● 1 Corinthians 13:1-13 is the chapter of love. It describes exactly what love is. Read this chapter with your group. Take time to talk about each attribute of love. What is one attribute that each of your kids need to work on from this list? How can they improve in this area? What makes it hard for them? Do they think God can help them with this?

WWW.POPMUSIC.TODAY

1. What's your opinion?

   My favorite **music group** or **performer** is—

   My favorite **song** is—

   My favorite **radio station** is—

2. **Circle** the amount of time you spend listening to music on an average day.

   none
   5 minutes
   30 minutes
   1 hour
   2 hours
   3 hours
   4 hours
   8 hours
   all day

3. Think of your **favorite song** again. What is it about? Summarize the message of the song in one sentence.

4. Read the statements and decide if you think they're **true** or **false**—

   _____ If a song has questionable lyrics, it shouldn't be played on the radio.
   _____ Today's popular music is no worse than music from other times.
   _____ Christians should listen only to Christian music.
   _____ My parents let me listen to any kind of music I want to hear.
   _____ If Jesus were a teenager today, he would probably listen to the same music I listen to.
   _____ The influences of music really aren't that big of a deal.

5. What is your interpretation of what **Colossians 2:6-8** says about music?

WWW.POPMUSIC.TODAY [popular music]

THIS WEEK

It's a fact that young people and adults in the church value music differently. Most teenagers listen to different types of music than adults do. And that's okay! Most young people identify with their peer group by listening to the same music as their friends. This TalkSheet was designed to facilitate a balanced discussion in regard to pop music.

OPENER

Begin the discussion by listening to a few different pop music CDs. Ask the kids to bring in their favorite CDs. They like the volume turned up loud, so you may decide to humor them for this discussion, to help you—and them—better understand the music that saturates the youth culture.

If available, bring a few records you enjoyed as a teenager. Most young people are familiar with the music of the all decades, including the 1970's and 1980's.

It is important to introduce this discussion in a positive way, without your young people thinking that you're criticizing their music. Try to be objective and listen to their thoughts and opinions.

THE DISCUSSION, BY THE NUMBERS

1. Have the kids share their favorites and tell why they chose them. Tally the results on a poster board or whiteboard and find out what performers, songs, and radio stations get the most votes.

2. Find out what time of day your kids listen to music—before school, during lunch, only on weekends, etc. Do they listen mostly to CDs? A portable CD player? The radio? Compare how much time they spend listening to music with how much time they spend doing other things, such as watching TV, working, doing homework, hanging out with friends, being with their families, and doing devotions.

3. This may show them that many don't even know the message of certain songs. Most people are passive listeners and don't realize what the words are saying! Discuss their favorite songs—do they contain questionable lyrics? What is the message in the song? Does the song talk about moral issues?

4. Have your kids take turns reading these aloud and find out what they think about each one. Hang on to your own comments until the wrap up.

5. Ask a few volunteers to read their applications of these verses to their music. Then discuss why God created music—he wanted us to enjoy it and use it to glorify him. Talk about what kinds of music God would approve of and what he wouldn't like. Point out that he'd want the music they hear to build us up and encourage us.

THE CLOSE

Teenagers spend millions of dollars on music CDs every year. It's important to encourage them to be aware of the kinds of music they listen to and how the music may influence them. It isn't wrong to like pop (or swing, rap, country, or anything else, for that matter), but it's wrong for Christians to spend time and money on anything that doesn't uphold the values of God.

A few suggested questions for them to ask themselves are, "Does this music draw me to or away from God?"; "What is this song telling me about my beliefs?"; and "Does the song support or oppose Christian values?" Challenge them to pay closer attention to the songs they listen to and to keep these questions in mind.

Brainstorm with your group some mainstream and Christian bands that are fun to listen to. Remember that it's not easy to label a band as "Christian"—there is so much crossover today. Encourage them to listen to the lyrics of the songs. What are they filling their heads with?

MORE

- Have the group study the Top 40 list of current hits and rate each song according to the content of the lyrics, the lifestyle of the artist, the music itself, and any other criteria you chose. Together rate each one and create your own Top 40 list.
- Encourage your kids to read the lyrics of the songs they listen to. It's surprising how much different a song is after you read the lyrics. You may want to read some lyrics for your kids, discuss them, and then play the song. How did reading the lyrics affect how they understood the song?
- Check out *Plugged In* magazine at www.family.org/pplace/pi/ (Focus on the Family) for the latest trends in music, TV, and movies. This is a useful resource for finding discussion information about news and reviews. Also, check out www.YouthSpecialties.com for information and links to finding discussion topics and latest news on teen culture.

GOT THE LOOK?

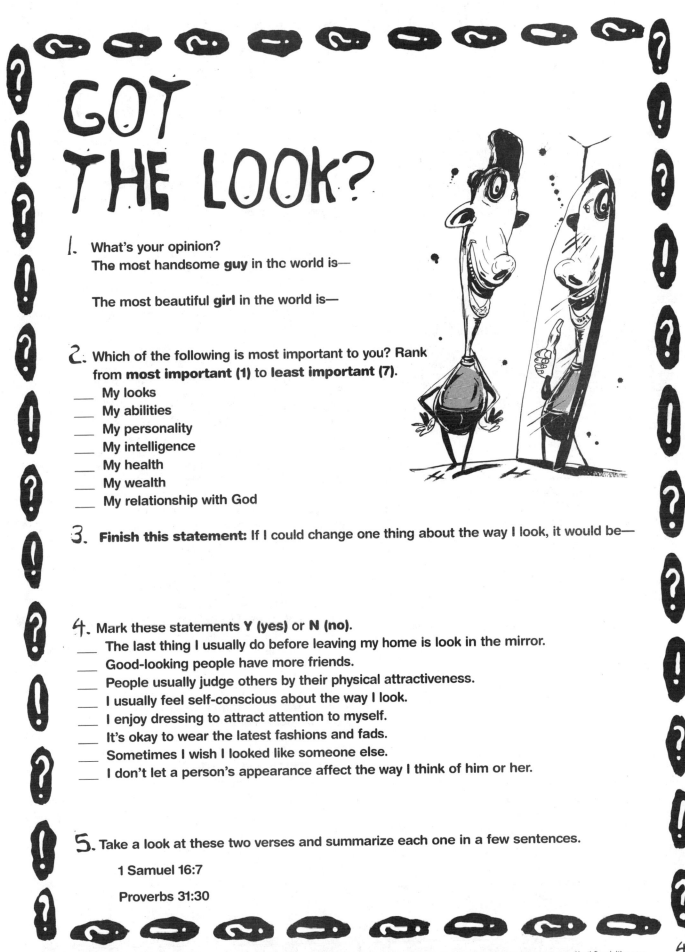

1. **What's your opinion?**
   The most handsome **guy** in the world is—

   The most beautiful **girl** in the world is—

2. Which of the following is most important to you? Rank
   from **most important (1)** to **least important (7)**.
   ___ My looks
   ___ My abilities
   ___ My personality
   ___ My intelligence
   ___ My health
   ___ My wealth
   ___ My relationship with God

3. **Finish this statement:** If I could change one thing about the way I look, it would be—

4. Mark these statements **Y (yes)** or **N (no)**.
   ___ The last thing I usually do before leaving my home is look in the mirror.
   ___ Good-looking people have more friends.
   ___ People usually judge others by their physical attractiveness.
   ___ I usually feel self-conscious about the way I look.
   ___ I enjoy dressing to attract attention to myself.
   ___ It's okay to wear the latest fashions and fads.
   ___ Sometimes I wish I looked like someone else.
   ___ I don't let a person's appearance affect the way I think of him or her.

5. Take a look at these two verses and summarize each one in a few sentences.

   1 Samuel 16:7

   Proverbs 31:30

49

GOT THE LOOK? [p h y s i c a l   a p p e a r a n c e]

THIS WEEK

Looking good is one of the biggest pressures among youth today—on the TV, radio, from friends, parents, boyfriends or girlfriends, the Internet, and more. It's no wonder that American girls are victims of eating disorders such as bulimia and anorexia. We are a society obsessed with looking good and fitting in. This TalkSheet gives your kids the chance to talk about physical appearances and discuss how their attitude affects them as Christians.

OPENER

Since the media is the number one influence on our looks, ask each person to cut out at least two pictures from magazines or newspapers that emphasize physical appearance. You can either do this within the group or have them bring pictures from home. What advertisements, articles, pictures, or statistics can they find?

Then take a look at each example and talk about how each one deals with physical appearance. Point out that in most ads, it's the looks of the person that sells the product. What does the picture show? How does that make the reader feel? What is the solution?

You may also want to talk about other media influences that stress good looks, like TV shows or movies. How can your kids keep a healthy perspective of themselves in a culture that idolizes the beautiful people? How can they resist the pressures to look and feel good without going overboard?

THE DISCUSSION, BY THE NUMBERS

1. Who does the group think has the look? Let them discuss why they chose the people they did.

2. Nobody (most likely) will put their looks as number one. They might put something else and some will list their relationship with God first. Ask the kids how much time each day they spend on their appearances. How long does it take them to look good? It's probably a lot more time than they spend with God!

3. Everyone has something that they don't like about how they look. Maybe share something that you would like to change about your own physical appearance and let others in the group to do the same. Point out that everyone—even the most famous movie stars—think that their looks need a change. But it's our individual looks that make us unique and special.

4. Since personal appearance can be hard to talk about, bring up these statements in a general way. Don't ask for personal examples—a few

might come out later. And don't be afraid to deal with the hurt, anger, and frustration many of your kids feel about their appearances. Each of your kids will have hang-ups about their looks and that's okay. They are all human and God made us different. Without glossing over their concerns, remind them that they were created by a God who made them unique in their own way. And, while some people might have better looks, they are all loved the same by God.

5. Have the group summarize these two passages and ask for examples of how the verses fit into their lives. How does God want us to think of ourselves? Can they be happy with our looks when they always want to change them? How can one be content with her or her looks?

THE CLOSE

There may be a lot to wrap up with this one! Emphasize that it's okay to want to look good and to take care of our bodies. But they shouldn't become obsessed with how they look. God wants us to take care of ourselves, both inside and outside. That means we can look good on the outside, but what's going on inside of us? Are we spending time on our character—who we are and what we believe? Are we letting God work in our hearts and minds? How can we balance wanting to look good outside and becoming better people, too?

MORE

● How do people try to change their physical appearance? Brainstorm with your group and make a list of ways that people alter how they look. For example—fad diets, plastic surgery, liposuction, steroids, weight lifting, and eating disorders. How do these change how people feel about themselves? Are these cures for a good self-esteem or not? What would God say about spending money and time on these things?

● Have the kids list three attributes that they like about themselves—are they outgoing? friendly? loving toward others? dedicated to their schoolwork? upbeat? Challenge them to pick one inner look that they want to improve and encourage them to set a goal for themselves. Have them write it down, put it in a self-addressed envelope, and send it to them later.

SO, WHAT'S THE DIFFERENCE?

1. How would you complete this? Circle one.
   For me, living as a Christian is—

   easy   hard   impossible

2. Is this statement **true** or **false**?
   If you don't act like a Christian, then you aren't a Christian.

3. Check which actions below you think a Christian would do—
   - ❑ Wear the latest style of clothes
   - ❑ Copy whatever your friends do
   - ❑ Stand up and defend your beliefs
   - ❑ Listen to the advice of your parents
   - ❑ Go to church
   - ❑ Witness to others by your actions and words
   - ❑ Care only about people who will care about you
   - ❑ Get good grades
   - ❑ Watch whatever is popular on TV
   - ❑ Say things you think others want to hear
   - ❑ Listen to God's word by reading the Bible
   - ❑ Make fun of the weird kids at school

4. Ramiro goes to church every Sunday and is a leader in his youth group. All the adults at church are proud of Ramiro because he's "such a fine Christian young man." When Ramiro goes away to school, however, none of his friends even know he's a Christian, because he acts just like everyone else.

   What is your opinion of Ramiro?

5. Which of the following verses warn against **hypocrisy**?

   Matthew 6:1   Matthew 7:15   Matthew 11:28   Matthew 23:1-4   Matthew 25:40

SO. WHAT'S THE DIFFERENCE? [h y p o c r i s y]

THIS WEEK

As kids get older they start to think more reflectively. They begin to observe and analyze how they and others live their lives. Adolescence is an important time for teenagers to develop their own ideals and set of morals. This TalkSheet gives you several options for discussing how your kids form and live out their Christian beliefs and values.

OPENER

The following skit (or a variation of it) may work as an intro—

BRIAN: Hi, Tom! How are you doing?

TOM: Not too good, Brian. I've got a big test in math tomorrow and I'm not ready for it.

BRIAN: Hey, I'm really good in math. I'll help you study anytime you want. Just say the word, and I'll be there. What are best friends for anyway?

TOM: Hey, that's great. I really appreciate that! How about tonight, so I can cram for the test. Say around seven?

BRIAN: Ummm, sorry. Can't make it. I'm busy tonight.

TOM: Oh. Well, uh, how about tomorrow morning—early, before school?

BRIAN: No way, man! My eyes don't focus until after lunch!

TOM: Oh. Well, thanks anyway, I guess. See you later.

BRIAN: You bet! And good luck on the test.

After the skit, ask your kids what they thought of Brian. Would they like to have Brian as a friend? Why or why not? They'll probably point out that Brian said one thing and did another. This is a good lead-in for a discussion on hypocrisy.

THE DISCUSSION, BY THE NUMBERS

1. Have the kids share their completed sentences with each other. Discuss the fact that the Christian life isn't easy to live and it never will be. It can real hard sometimes—it's not surprising that Christians blow it most of the time. But that doesn't mean we should stop trying to do live according to our beliefs as Christians.

2. You may want to raise this major theological issue—does salvation come by faith or by good works? Ask for your kids' opinions, but don't let the discussion go too far. Point out that God loves us for who we are—no one is the perfect Christian. Our goal is to live each day like Christ wants us to, even if we do mess up.

3. Talk about each statement and ask why the kids checked the ones they did. This is a good time to discuss Christian conduct.

4. Ask the kids to share their opinion of Ramiro. Why do they think Ramiro lives two different lives? What are some ways that he can let his friends know that he's a Christian? How would they expect Ramiro's life to be different?

5. Ask the kids to look up the verses and read those that deal with hypocrisy. Have them explain the meanings and paraphrase how the verses apply to their lives.

THE CLOSE

Close the discussion with a challenge to your group members to practice what they preach. Leave room to talk about God's forgiveness. Also, you may want to discuss tolerance—within reason—for other Christians. God doesn't expect others to be perfect and they shouldn't either.

Communicate that it's easy to fake others out and to pretend to be something you're not. But God knows our hearts. He knows us better than we know ourselves—we'll never fool him.

MORE

● What can each of your kids do during the next week to put their faith into practice? Ask them to write their ideas on a 3x5 card (kind of like a pledge) and give them to you. Then, a week or so later, go through the cards and talk about how they did. What was easy or hard about living their faith? What long-term changes can they shoot for?

● Or you may want to talk with your kids about how tolerant they should be of others behaviors. At what point should they draw the line? Possibly have a role-play situation in which one kid sees another doing something irritating. How are they going to handle the situation? What is hard about confronting fellow Christians about their behavior?

● On a large whiteboard or poster board, draw two columns labeled "Christian" and "Others." Brainstorm with your youths what characteristics or stereotypes there are of Christians and others. Discuss how Christians are portrayed in the media—on TV shows and movies. How can your kids live in the world without making others feel inferior? How would there lives be different if they weren't Christians?

THE DEVIL MADE ME DO IT

1. Which one do you think is the **absolute worst**? Why?

- ❑ Telling a lie
- ❑ Cheating on a test
- ❑ Stealing from your parents
- ❑ Chain-smoking
- ❑ Looking at porno magazines or Web sites
- ❑ Faking the flu to get out of school
- ❑ Doing drugs

- ❑ Backstabbing a friend
- ❑ Cussing out a teammate
- ❑ Plagiarizing information off the Internet
- ❑ Drinking alcohol
- ❑ Hitting a sibling
- ❑ Going too far with physical intimacy
- ❑ Shoplifting

2. How would you answer each item?

a. I'm tempted to do bad things—
- ❑ more now than I used to be.
- ❑ about the same now as I used to be.
- ❑ less now than I used to be.

b. When I give in to temptation, I usually feel—
- ❑ ashamed of myself.
- ❑ proud of myself.
- ❑ okay about myself.
- ❑ nothing.

c. Most of the time, when I'm tempted—
- ❑ I think about it a long time.
- ❑ I give in right away.
- ❑ I try to ignore the temptation.
- ❑ I read my Bible and pray.

3. True or **false**—
a. Sometimes God tempts you as a test, to see if you will resist._____
b. It's a sin to be tempted to do bad things._____
c. Christians are tempted as often as non-Christians._____
d. Some temptations are too hard to resist._____
e. Temptation comes from the devil._____
f. If you give in to temptation, it's the devil's fault._____

4. Complete the sentences below, using what you learn from reading the following Bible verses **Psalm 119:11, Luke 22:46, 1 Corinthians 10:13**, and **James 4:7**.
One way to resist temptation is to—
Another way is to—
I know that when I am tempted, God will—
If I resist the devil's temptation, I know the devil will—

THE DEVIL MADE ME DO IT [temptation]

THIS WEEK

Temptations are everywhere for both teenagers and adults. As your kids get more independence from their parents and approach adulthood, they'll face temptations that they never have before. They'll also realize how temptations can lead to feelings of guilt and failure. Use this TalkSheet to discuss temptation with your group in a supportive, encouraging way.

OPENER

This intro will be sure to get things going. Have your kids write out temptations that they—or teenagers their age—face in their lives (don't have them write names). Then collect the pieces of paper.

Your kids will role-play the temptations that come with each of these situations. Start by asking for three volunteers—one a devil, another an angel, and the third as a person being tempted (the tempted). Ask the tempted to sit in a chair with the devil on one side, the angel on the other. Pick a situation and read it out loud. Then the angel and devil must work against each other to influence the tempted's decision. You can rotate participants with different situations to get everyone involved.

Afterwards, ask the group how they felt as the person who was being tempted. Which, the angel or the devil, was easier to listen to? What pressures were hard to resist? How did they balance their values against what they wanted to do?

THE DISCUSSION, BY THE NUMBERS

1. Try to keep this one general—don't expect your kids to reveal their answers. Go the roundabout way and ask them how many items they checked. Ask them which ones they feel teenagers in general struggle with the most.

2. When asking them to share their answers, don't force anyone to participate. Point out that teens face temptation now more than they did ever have. Brainstorm ways to resist temptation when discussing the second sentence. After the last sentence, explain to the group that guilt and shame are normal feelings. Communicate that if they are sorry for what they've done and ask for forgiveness, God forgives and takes away the guilt.

3. Temptation is Satan's way of stealing people away from God. Satan cannot make your kids do anything, so they can't blame Satan for their sins. Satan is extremely powerful and he tempts people in their weaknesses. God never tempts people—that's Satan at work.

4. How did your kids complete the sentences on temptation? Talk about how Jesus dealt with temptation and what your kids can do in their lives to avoid certain situations.

THE CLOSE

Temptation is part of being human. Everyone has been created by God with a free will—they are responsible for their choices. And, the choices they make today will affect them in the future. Even though they can make choices, they must be aware of the consequences that may follow.

How can your group members strengthen their faith and resist temptation? What are some ways to protect themselves from Satan's schemes? The more firmly rooted they are in Christ, the more power they'll have from the Holy Spirit. God gives his followers tools to resist the devil—reading the Bible, memorizing verses, getting involved in youth group, hanging out with Christian friends, and communicating regularly with God through prayer. The best way to resist temptation is to stay close to Christ—the only man in history who has ever beat the devil on his own turf. Christ can give them the strength to make the right choices. You may want to read a few Bible passages to take this further—the temptation of Christ (Matthew 4:1-11) and the armor of God and spiritual warfare (Ephesians 6:10-18).

MORE

● What is one temptation in particular that each of your kids struggles with? Ask the group the following questions to think about—what is this temptation? Are there certain times when they are tempted more than other times? Do certain people tempt them more than others? What can they do to avoid this temptation from now on?

● On a large poster board or whiteboard, have your kids list specific temptations that teenagers face. Some of these include pornography, premarital sex, drinking, and drug abuse. Use these examples to set up case scenarios of a kid who is tempted and must chose what to do. Talk about the consequences if he or she gives in to the temptation. What may happen if the kid resists? What if they give in? What impact with this have in a month? A year? Longer? You may want to play devil's advocate to get them thinking.

GOD IN A BOD

1. What words below describe Jesus? **Circle** those that do and X those that don't.

meek	humble	honest
strong	mysterious	awesome
strange	boring	wimpy
sad	friendly	loving
fun	happy	God
tough	angry	caring
cool	smart	perfect

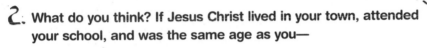

2. What do you think? If Jesus Christ lived in your town, attended your school, and was the same age as you—

- Would he be **popular** or **unpopular**?

- Where would he go to **church**?

- What kind of **music** would he listen to?

- What would he do **after school**?

- What **TV shows** would he watch, if any?

- Would he like your **youth group**, if he attended?

3. If someone asked you why you believed in Jesus, how would you respond?

   What would you say if they argued with you?

4. Christ asked his disciples, **"Who do people say that I am?"** (Matthew 16:13, author's paraphrase). Find out what each of the following Bible verses says about Christ, then complete each of the sentences.

   Matthew 16:16   Jesus is—

   John 3:16-17   Jesus is—

   John 10:30   Jesus is—

   Colossians 1:13-23   Jesus is—

GOD IN A BOD [Jesus Christ]

THIS WEEK

Most of your kids may have learned about Jesus Christ through Bible stories and in Sunday school. But do they really understand who he is? The creator of the universe was God—in human form! He was born as a baby, just like every other person. This TalkSheet focuses on Christ's attributes and how to get to know him better.

OPENER

On a large sheet of white paper or a whiteboard have the kids make a list of words they think describe Jesus—his physical looks, his spiritual nature, his personality traits, et cetera. Where do they get these ideas? From the Bible? From pictures or models of Christ in church or in stores? What does society say about Jesus? How do they describe him? What do your kids hear about Jesus at school?

Or try this. How well does your group know the life of Christ? Give the group a list of events in the life of Christ such as his baptism, the Sermon on the Mount, key miracles, parables. Divide the group teams to compete and arrange the events chronologically.

THE DISCUSSION, BY THE NUMBERS

1. Have the kids share the words they circled and the ones they crossed out. What reasons to they have for their answers? Are there any other words that describe Jesus?

2. What kids of person would Jesus be if he were living today in their town? Put aside the "Jesus in the carpenter shop" image and portray him as a modern-day teenager. This may be challenging—remind them that there's no right or wrong answer. What ideas from Bible verses support their answers, if any?

3. This is a heavy question for some kids, especially those who are new Christians. Don't expect them to open up easily. This may be a good time to share your thoughts about what Jesus means to you. You may want to follow up with a question like, "How does believing in Jesus make a difference in your life?"

4. Have several kids share their completed sentences and discuss the character traits of Christ. What traits of Christ do your kids admire the most? Which ones do your kids need to work on?

THE CLOSE

Christ works in each person differently. You may want to share what he has done for you. How has a relationship with him changed your life? The blind man Jesus healed put it simply in John 9:25, "One thing I do know. I was blind but now I see!" Explain that your kids can let Christ change their lives—are they willing? Will they let Christ live in them and work in their hearts? The only way to understand Jesus is know him better.

Point out that Christ is their friend—not a remote autocratic being in heaven. He is someone who will stay close to them. He understands their situations, needs, desires, temptations, and struggles because he lived on earth as a human. Invite your group to start a personal relationship with Jesus if they haven't already. What will they lose? Nothing. They'll gain the best friend they've ever had.

MORE

● This lesson can't cover everything about Christ. You may want to start a Bible study or small group on the life of Christ. Several materials, including *Creative Bible Lessons on the Life of Christ* (Doug Fields) are available from Youth Specialties. Check out the YS Web page (www.YouthSpecialties.com) for more information and links for more materials.

● How is Christ is portrayed by the media—on the Internet, in movies, or on TV? Ask your group to do some outside research to find some examples. They'll most likely be able to find both good and bad ones. Discuss the examples they found and how society depicts Christ. Are these accurate examples of Jesus? What do these examples say about Christianity and religion?

● You may want to use this lesson to explain the difference between God and Jesus. Some of your kids may wonder how Jesus can be God is he's God's son. This is tough to explain in simple terms! Be careful not to get too theological, but take the time to explain the Trinity and the relationship between God, Jesus, and the Holy Spirit. Take a look at the TalkSheet "Got Spirit"? (page 103) for more discussion questions, explanations, and activities.

EYES ON THE STARS

1. Who was one of your heroes when you were **young**?

   Who is one of your heroes **now**?

2. Name someone **famous** in each of the following categories.
   A famous music star—
   A famous athlete—
   A famous politician—
   A famous writer—
   A famous actor or actress—

3. What would you consider to be heroic? **Check three** of the following.
   - ❏ Teaching Sunday school
   - ❏ Cleaning up my room
   - ❏ Being on the cover of *Teen People* magazine
   - ❏ Volunteering at a nursing home
   - ❏ Winning the state lottery
   - ❏ Wearing the right kind of clothes
   - ❏ Getting a part in a movie
   - ❏ Writing a hit song
   - ❏ Telling the truth when it's easier to lie
   - ❏ Being voted my team's MVP

4. What do you think?
   The person I most want to be like when I grow up is—
   Why?

5. Match the following verses with the correct letter.
   1. Joshua 9:9-10
   2. 1 Samuel 17:51
   3. 1 Kings 4:29-34
   4. Proverbs 31:10-31
   5. Matthew 4:23-25

   a. a defeated hero
   b. a wise hero
   c. a heroine
   d. a famous God
   e. a hero people followed

EYES ON THE STARS [heroes]

THIS WEEK

Media has the power to create heroes and heroines. But these celebrities—shaped by TV, sports, movies, or music videos—aren't necessarily heroic. Sometimes their moral behaviors aren't ones that they'd like our kids to follow. Heroes and heroines these days can be anyone from professional golfers to world leaders. They are heroes because people admire and respect them. This TalkSheet will help you discuss why they look up to certain people and what a hero is.

OPENER

Try this charades-type game! Before your meeting, write names of some heroes or heroines in large letters on individual pieces of 8½ x 11 paper or Post-It notes. You can include different kinds of heroes including (but not limited to)—

- Superheroes—Superman, X-Men, Spiderman, Batman, and so on.
- Sports champions—Tiger Woods, Michael Jordan, Andre Agassi, Brandi Chastain, Marion Jones, and so on.
- Actors—Julia Roberts, Jim Carrey, Robin Williams, Cameron Diaz, and so on.
- Music stars—Madonna, Dave Matthews, Garth Brooks, Faith Hill, Britney Spears, and so on.

Once you've got these on paper, don't let your kids see them. Split your group up into two (or more) teams. Each team will take turns having a volunteer come up to the front. You'll then stick a piece of paper or Post-It on the volunteer's back or forehead (a hat with duct tape on the front works well). Don't let the volunteer see the name of the hero! In a given amount of time (a minute or so), the other group members have to describe the hero or heroine on the paper to the volunteer—without saying the name of the person in any context. If the volunteer can guess the name of the hero, the team gets a point.

THE DISCUSSION, BY THE NUMBERS

1. What heroes or heroines did your youth have when they were younger? How about now? How many of them still have the same hero? Have them share why the person is important to them and considered to be hero-worthy.

2. Discuss the difference between a famous person today—known as a celebrity—and a hero or heroine. A celebrity is a creation of media publicity. Heroes earn their titles and they often reflect on the merits of what they have done. Heroes take moral positions and live by exemplary standards.

3. Point out that heroic deeds don't always bring fame. Fame has nothing to do with morality today—instead it deals with what is popular and trendy. And remind them that a heroic act may be something as insignificant—even cleaning up their room—because it is an act of discipline, obedience, and respect.

4. Ask the kids to share the people they chose. You'll most likely get a variety of answers. Take this time to talk about their role models. What traits or characteristics should good role models have? Are their heroes good role models for them?

5. These verses deal with heroes and heroines in the Bible. Discuss with your kids what made each of them heroic and how God used their deeds.

THE CLOSE

Everyone has a hero—but they should be smart about who they choose. The apostle Paul said, "Imitate me." He wasn't boasting! He was saying, "I'll be your hero. You need a hero who acts as Jesus wants him to do. Imitate me as I imitate Christ" (1 Corinthians 3:17, author's paraphrase). Don't model yourself after anyone who doesn't reflect the values and high standards of the Christian faith.

Challenge your kids to choose their heroes wisely—and also to live heroically through their actions and examples. Some of your kids think they're nobody—encourage them to believe they can do great things for the kingdom of God.

MORE

- The Bible is full of people who would be considered heroic. Have the group find examples or stories of heroes in the Bible—who would they consider hero-worthy (besides Jesus, of course!)? What actions or characteristics make them heroes of faith? What can they admire about this person? What does God consider heroic?
- Hold a contest to see who can find the most interesting facts about their hero or heroine. Challenge them to look on the Internet, in magazines, or wherever they can find some information. And whoever brings the most unique, quirky, or interesting fact about their hero gets a prize. Have your kids vote on the best one. Did this info change the way that they feel about their heroes? How?

WHAT, ME WORRY?

1. **Mark** an *X* next to the things you worry about.

___ What others think of me
___ What grades I get
___ How I look
___ Who I'm going to date
___ What kind of job I'll have someday
___ Who really likes me at school
___ If I'll make the sports team
___ When there will be another war
___ When I'll die

___ When my friends will have another fight
___ If my parents will stay together
___ When I'll be abused again
___ When my parent will get help with an addiction.
___ How I'm doing in my walk with Christ
___ What the world will be like when I'm older
___ Other—

2. Check which one makes more sense to you.
The more I worry about something—
❏ the worse it becomes.
❏ the better it becomes.
❏ the more I realize worry it doesn't change a thing.
❏ the worse it gets in my mind.

3. What would you say to a friend who was worried about—

a. Mom and Dad getting a divorce?

b. failing a class?

c. getting dumped by a boyfriend or girlfriend?

d. getting a new—but bad—haircut?

4. How can a person get rid of worry?

5. Look up the following verses then summarize them in your own words.

Romans 8:28

Philippians 4:6-7

1 Peter 5:7

WHAT, ME WORRY? [w o r r y]

THIS WEEK

Adolescents have way too much to worry about—their looks, relationships, grades, their future, and more. Today's teenager deals with more stress and tension than ever before. This TalkSheet will help your group talk about their worries and insecurities and how their faith can help them through.

OPENER

Start with a worry-version of the game Pictionary. Have your kids write down some random, funny worries that they deal with or think about. Some possibilities include—having body odor, getting a pimple on the nose, flunking a math test, not knowing how to kiss, not knowing your fly is open, not being able to get to sleep, going to the dentist, or passing gas. Collect them and have volunteers from each team take turns drawing these worries. The rest of the group tries to guess what kind of worry is being drawn and the team with the most points wins.

THE DISCUSSION, BY THE NUMBERS

1. Some of your kids maybe won't want to open up right away, so start them off by talking about some of the things that worried you as a teenager. Use a whiteboard or poster board to write down worries and insecurities that they face at school, home, church, work, wherever.

2. Your kids will find logical answers to these worries. Point out that worrying really doesn't help make a situation better. But sometimes worry is okay—it can motivate them to do things that are good. For example, a student who worries about gaining weight starts a workout program.

3. Have the kids share their advice with the others. You may wish to role-play the situations, with one student acting as the worrier and the other giving advice.

4. Brainstorm some different solutions to worrying. List them on a whiteboard for everyone to see. Define the difference between worry—that doesn't change things—and concern—that motivates change. Communicate that worry is a waste of emotional energy that can be better spend solving a problem or finding a solution.

5. After reading these verses, talk about what God thinks about worrying. Explain that worrying is actually taking situations into our own hands and trying to control our lives. Encourage your kids to give the situations over to God instead of worrying, and to ask for his peace and guidance.

THE CLOSE

The English word worry comes from the German word *wurgen*, meaning "to choke." Worry, in a sense, is mental agony and can weaken the soul.

It's normal and healthy to have worries, but it can be destructive and self-defeating. It's useless to worry about things that you can't control.

Help your kids realize Christians don't have to worry about the past or the future—both are in God's hands. Jesus says repeatedly in Matthew 6:25-34 that we have nothing to worry about. Whether we know it or not, God is taking care of us.

Brainstorm ways that your youths can deal with their worries. Encourage them to talk about their worries with someone else—a friend, a parent, and another respected adult—someone who is willing to listen. Let them know you are available to listen and help.

MORE

● What happens when people get wrapped up in worry? Have your kids list and talk about what worry does to us physically and the outcomes of worry. Address issues like physical stress, anxiety, depression, and what happens when people can't deal with their worries—like suicide and abusing alcohol or drugs. Communicate that worry is more than just a spiritual battle—it's a mental battle, too. What can they do to help themselves deal with their worries?

● Have your kids find examples of things that people their age worry about. They can find examples all over—in teenage magazines, on the Internet, radio, song lyrics, and more. Help them understand that everyone has worries—even famous athletes and celebrities.

● Time for a little Q & A! Ask your group member to write down (anonymously) things they worry about. Pick them out and read them aloud. What advice or encouragement do they have for each other? What suggestions to you or other adults have? Where can they go to get more information?

YOU MAKE ME SO MAD

1. From the situations listed, **circle three** that would make you really mad.
   a. Someone swears at you.
   b. Your parents ground you.
   c. You flunk a test.
   d. You have to do two hours of homework.
   e. Someone steals your bike.
   f. Your mom asks you to help with the dishes, and you're already in a bad mood.
   g. Someone threatens you.
   h. A friend talks about you behind your back.
   i. Your parents blame you for something you didn't do.
   j. A sibling takes something of yours without asking.
   h. Your boyfriend or girlfriend dumps you.

2. Answer the following questions about anger.

   When my **mom** gets mad, she—

   When my **dad** gets mad, he—

   When **I** get mad, I—

3. Darrin is standing patiently in the cafeteria line when two guys push their way into the line, cutting in front of Darrin. He's shoved off balance, falls down, and loses his place in line. The two guys just laugh at him.

   How would you feel if you were Darrin?

   What would you do if you were Darrin?

4. Decide what's right from the following statements, and write **Y (yes)** or **N (no)**.
   ___ a. I have the right to be angry with someone who hurts me.
   ___ b. People who lose their temper are immature.
   ___ c. Anger is a sin.
   ___ d. Christians should show their anger differently from non-Christians.
   ___ e. Don't get mad, get even.

5. Choose one of the following Bible verses to rewrite in your own words.

   Proverbs 14:17

   Proverbs 15:1

   Ephesians 4:26-27

YOU MAKE ME SO MAD [anger]

THIS WEEK

Anger is a powerful emotion and a difficult one to handle, especially for teenagers. It has been said that "anger, like fire, finally dies out—but not before it leaves a path of destruction." Most young people don't know how to deal with anger. This TalkSheet gives your group a chance talk about anger, healthy solutions, and how a Christian should handle it.

OPENER

Before the meeting, ask one of your group's members to help you with the intro. Tell the kid that you are going to role-play anger and he or she needs to pretend to annoy you. During the opening of the meeting, the music, the announcements, and the games, your volunteer should constantly disrupt the meeting. Then just before the discussion begins, pretend you have lost your patience and blow your top. Tell the student actor to get out and never come back, in no uncertain terms. Let the group hang for a minute, let your "anger" cool, and then let them into your ruse. Did they actually think you were angry? What did they think when you blew up?

THE DISCUSSION, BY THE NUMBERS

1. Allow enough time for the kids to share the items they circled. Communicate that they don't have to let other people or circumstances make them mad—they do have a choice. Anger is an issue of self-control, which is hard to have sometimes!

2. Oftentimes, your kids handle anger the same way our parents do. This item may help them understand their own reactions. Let individuals talk about the different ways in which they and their parents handle anger.

3. You can use this attention-getter to role-play a true-life situation with the group. Ask the kids to think of their own frustrating situations to solve and discuss.

4. Many young people have difficulty expressing anger. They either hold it inside or let it out in destructive ways. Some may feel anger is a sin. Anger is an emotional reaction—not a sin. It's what they do with the anger that counts. Discuss healthy ways to deal with anger—but don't gloss over the fact that it's okay get mad sometimes. Especially if that anger can lead to positive outcomes, like fixing a friendship, mending a relationship, or understanding a situation better.

5. Ask several kids to share their paraphrased verses and apply them to their own lives. Discuss

that Jesus experienced anger, too (Matthew 21:12-13). Even God gets angry (Joshua 23:16)! Also, point out that God gives us peace and is able to take anger away. Challenge your youth to ask God to help them deal with their anger and ask him to fill them with his peace.

THE CLOSE

Norman Vincent Peale said, "The next time you feel a surge of anger, say to yourself, 'Is this really worth what it's going to do to me and another, emotionally? I will make a fool of myself. I may hurt someone I love, or I might lose a friend.'"

Challenge your group members to deal with their anger in healthy ways. Encourage them to take some time to cool off. Assure them their angry feelings are not sinful—it's the reaction that they need to control.

Also, you may want to discuss what happens when people let their anger go too far. Some of your kids may have abusive parents, broken homes, or substance abusers in their families. It's crucial to communicate that it is never acceptable for a parent, boyfriend, or other person to hit them out of anger. Remind them that if they or a friend is ever in an abusive situation, they must seek help from a trusted adult—a teacher, school counselor, or pastor. Assure them that you are there for them as a confidential source of support and help. For more information and links on physical abuse, check out the National Exchange Club Foundation (www.preventchildabuse.com) or the American Humane Association (www.americanhumane.org).

MORE

- You may want to take some time to talk about the impact of anger in our society. List some current situations in the news that relate to anger, such as examples of school violence, gang activity, rape, or other crimes. Communicate that ours is a very pressured society—there are so many expectations some people can't deal with. What role can your kids play to be peacemakers among their peers and families?

- Have your kids surf the Internet for information on hate groups—they are everywhere. Some include skinheads, neo-Nazis, and white supremacists. You may be surprised at what your kids already know about these—they are nearly in every school across the country. Take some time to learn more about these if you don't know anything about these groups. Discuss the motives behind these groups, what issues they are angry about, and what your kids can do to deal with these groups.

PG (PARENTAL GUIDANCE)

1. If you had enough money to buy any **three** of the following for your parent or guardian, **which ones would you buy?**

   ❏ more love
   ❏ more patience
   ❏ better health
   ❏ sense of humor

   ❏ fewer worries
   ❏ better looks
   ❏ more time with me
   ❏ more faith in God

   ❏ more fun
   ❏ more money
   ❏ better job
   ❏ more energy

2. Place an *X* on the line below, indicating which direction you are moving in your relationship with your parents.

   Closer to parents   **Away from parents**

3. If you were one of the adults who are responsible for you—

   What would you do more?

   What would you do less?

4. What do you think—**T (true)** or **F (false)**?
   My parents—
   ___ are clueless about my problems.
   ___ fight with each other a lot.
   ___ like to have fun with me.
   ___ don't trust me.
   ___ like my friends.
   ___ won't let me do what my friends do.
   ___ blame me for too much stuff.
   ___ treat me like a child.
   ___ give me as much money as I want.
   ___ pay little attention to my needs.
   ___ expect way too much of me.
   ___ don't care what I do or when.

5. Which of these Bible verses go with the statements below?
   1. Proverbs 3:11-12
   2. Proverbs 20:11
   3. Ephesians 6:2-3
   4. Colossians 3:20-21
   5. Hebrews 11:23

   a. Obedience pleases God.
   b. Honor your parents and live long.
   c. The Lord disciplines his children.
   d. Parents protect children.
   e. Actions show the real you.

PG (PARENTAL GUIDANCE) [parents]

THIS WEEK

As the kids in your group get older, they'll grow away from their parents and form their own identities. Most of them probably have started already! This can cause stress and rebellion at home. Parents sometimes come off as old-fashioned and too strict. This TalkSheet will help you discuss parent-teen relationships with your kids in a positive way—and hopefully help them see that parents and guardians are people, too!

Your kids may come from different types of families, including divorced homes, one-parent families, or foster homes. Be extra sensitive to this as you go through this session. Don't assume that all your kids have traditional two-parent homes.

OPENER

On a large sheet of poster board or on a whiteboard, have your kids write down some things that they'd change about their parents or guardians if they could. Jumpstart them if they need ideas—things like "give me more freedom," "don't force me to take piano lessons," and so on. If they don't want to get specific, that's okay.

On a second poster board, have your kids write down some things that their parents would like to change about them—their kids. Keep your kids on track—you might have a kid who writes, "nothing, I'm perfect."

Now compare the two lists. Point out that both parents and kids have faults and make mistakes—they are all humans! And point out that parent-child relationships are two-sided—parents and kids will see things differently, and that's okay. Remind them that respect is the key issue when dealing with parents. After all, they are being fed, clothed, driven, and paid for by their parents!

THE DISCUSSION, BY THE NUMBERS

1. This gets kids thinking about what their parents or guardians need the most. It'll also show you what your kids and their families value the most. Let volunteers share their choices.

2. Allow discussion about where the young people think their relationships with their parents are going. Some kids don't think it's cool to get along with their parents, others do. Maybe tell them a few things about your relationship with your parents (when you were younger, of course). How can they improve their relationships with their parents?

3. Emphasize the positive on this item and encourage them to think of the good things their parents do with them and for them. Don't let this turn into a gripe session.

4. Talk about each of these problem areas and watch for the ones where the most frequent response is *true*. With these, stop and ask the kids how they could change their situation. For instance, how can they earn their parents trust?

5. Read the verses and talk about how your kids can apply these to their home situations. What changes to they themselves need to make? What issues do they need to raise with their parents? What does God say about respecting parents?

THE CLOSE

Encourage your kids to see their parents as people, not just parents. Keep your closing comments upbeat and emphasize that relationships take work, even between parents and kids.

Remind them that God gave us adults to take care of us and they should be thankful—without them they wouldn't be here! Challenge your kids to look at situations from a different angle—from their parents' perspective.

And remind the group that God commands us in Exodus 20:12 to honor and obey our parents, even when they don't feel like it. This command—one of the Ten Commandments—comes with a promise, too. They won't regret loving and honoring our parents.

Finally, close with a prayer for everyone's parents, guardian, or caretaker and give thanks for them. Give the kids a few moments to pray silently for their relationships and struggles with their parents.

MORE

● Give your kids a parent quiz to do over the next week. To answer the questions, they'll have to talk with their parents to find out the answers. A few good questions to include are—How old were your parents when they first started dating? Where did they go on their first date? What were their majors in college? How did they feel when you were born? How did they celebrate their first anniversary?

● How do movies or TV shows deal with parent-teen relationships? You may want to show clips of movies or TV shows and discuss them with the group. What happened between the parent and teenager? How did they both handle the situation? Was it realistic? What would you or your parents have done differently?

HUNGER HURTS

1. What is your favorite **food**?

What is your favorite **soft drink**?

What is your favorite **dessert**?

2. Complete the sentences below by checking the ending that fits you.

I eat—
- ❑ one meal a day.
- ❑ two meals a day.
- ❑ three meals a day.
- ❑ more than three meals a day.
- ❑ three meals a day, plus snacks.
- ❑ whenever I feel hungry.

I eat—
- ❑ only what I know is good for me.
- ❑ anything that tastes good.
- ❑ mostly junk food.
- ❑ whatever my family eats.

I eat—
- ❑ less than the average person my age.
- ❑ more than the average person my age.
- ❑ the same as the average person my age.

When I'm hungry—
- ❑ I wait until the next meal.
- ❑ I have a snack.
- ❑ I go crazy!

3. Do you **agree** or **disagree**?

a. There are no hungry people in America.

b. It's their own fault if some people are hungry.

c. It's God's will for some people of the world to be hungry.

d. One shouldn't eat just for pleasure.

e. It's a sin to overeat.

f. There's nothing I can do to help the hungry people of the world.

4. **Match** each Bible verses with the correct statement.

1. Deuteronomy 14:28-29	a. The poor will always be around.
2. Matthew 25:34-36	b. The rich man and Lazarus will meet again after death.
3. Luke 16:19-26	c. Christians help others.
4. John 12:8	d. There's a reward for helping the poor.
5. Acts 11:28-30	e. God commands us to help.

HUNGER HURTS [world hunger]

THIS WEEK

Most American teenagers are out of touch with world hunger. They sometimes hear about it, or see pictures of starving people on the news or in magazines, but they can't relate with these people. Our society can't expect kids to understand poverty-stricken life. America is a wealthy society, and it has the world's highest rate of obesity. This TalkSheet was designed to help your youth think about their own eating habits in light of world hunger and what God has to say about this.

OPENER

You can introduce this a number of ways, depending on your group. If you usually have meetings in the evenings where you serve food—like pizza, soda, chips, cookies, or brownies—do something different for this meeting. People in poverty-stricken countries don't have a choice what they get to eat—they don't get yummy treats. So for this meeting, have whoever makes the food (that might be you) cook up only rice or chicken broth. Serve only one scoop of rice (no sugar or soy sauce on it) or a bowl of broth (without crackers) to each youth. Just one scoop and one cup of water. Explain to them that if they were living in a second or third world country, they wouldn't be complaining about eating rice (or broth) and fresh water. Let them think about that while they're craving hot cheese pizza! Okay, later on you can be nice and serve treats—but after the discussion.

Can't go without the pizza? There are posters and descriptive videos available at no or very low cost from organizations such as World Vision (www.wvi.org) or Compassion International (www.ci.org). These give real-life stories and pictures of the poverty and hunger in most second and third world countries. You may want to get one of these and show it to your group as an intro to this discussion.

THE DISCUSSION, BY THE NUMBERS

1. Who doesn't have a favorite food? You kids will have lots of answers to this one! Without sounding judgmental, point out that in most countries young people have no choice about what they eat. Most people there could never dream of tasting the wonderful variety of foods that they have.

2. Junior high and middle school kids are a hungry bunch. Their bodies are in a state of constant growth and need plenty of nourishment for healthy development. Let them share their responses with the group. Point out how important food is to them as well as to young people around the world.

3. Go over each item. You may want to focus on item b—some people believe that the people who are starving are to blame. Be sensitive to the ones in your group who are overweight, when looking at d and e. Their self-esteem is already suffering. Some may bring up dieting at this point—some of your young people may have problems in that area.

4. Take a look at these verses and ask the kids how they'd apply them to their lives. They may have some questions like why God allows hunger and why he blesses others.

THE CLOSE

Just because your kids can't go to Somalia, doesn't mean they can't help the starving there. Let them know they can actually make a difference. Tell the Bible story about the feeding of the five thousand (Mark 6:38-44) when Jesus used a small lunch to feed a multitude. In the same way, they can support those world relief organizations that God is using to feed the hungry—he will multiply our gift.

It's easy to take food for granted because it's always there. But food is a gift from God. You may want to end the session with a prayer for the hungry people of the world and to thank God for the blessing of food.

MORE

● You may want to organize a group fundraising activity for a Christian relief agency. Several ideas include a Saturday afternoon car wash, a pancake breakfast, garage sale, or service auction. Publicize that you are raising money for world hunger and use the opportunity to make others more aware of these issues.

● Challenge your kids to participate in a 24-hour world hunger fast. You can do this as a group in a number of ways. Some groups gather pledges from people and use the fast as a fundraiser. Other groups simply start the fast with a prayer time, fast for 24 hours, and then debrief with a healthy meal at the end. Make sure you do this at a good time of the year when it's healthy for your kids to participate (you don't want parents calling to complain that their child can't play soccer because he hasn't eaten anything!) So be sure to have parental support and involvement, too.

LIAR, LIAR

1. Who would you consider to be the most honest? Why?
   Check as many as you want.

   ❑ the President of the United States
   ❑ a door-to-door salesman
   ❑ a minister
   ❑ a celebrity in a TV commercial
   ❑ your parents
   ❑ a school counselor

   ❑ your best friend
   ❑ a teacher
   ❑ a music star
   ❑ a police officer
   ❑ your boyfriend or girlfriend
   ❑ you

2. What is a **white lie?**

3. Most would say the following are dishonest statements. **Rate** them from **most dishonest (1)** to the **least (10)**.

   ___ Lying to parents so you can go out.
   ___ Cheating on a test.
   ___ Keeping the money when a cashier gives you too much change.
   ___ Spreading a rumor when it's not true.
   ___ Making illegal copies of a CD or video tape.

   ___ Shoplifting a gift for someone.
   ___ Giving a fake excuse to a teacher.
   ___ Borrowing something and not returning it.
   ___ Protecting a friend by lying.
   ___ Giving **false** info about yourself in an online chatroom.

4. Natalie lied to her parents about where she spent the afternoon. She knew that if she told her parents the truth, they would be disappointed and angry. Her parents believed her and nothing more was said.

   What do you think of Natalie's actions?

   What would you do if you were Natalie?

5. Read the following Bible verses and decide if each one is an example of honesty or dishonesty.

   Genesis 12:10-13
   1 Samuel 12:1-5
   Amos 8:4-5

   Luke 19:5-8
   Acts 5:1-2
   2 Corinthians 8:19-21

From *Junior High-Middle School TalkSheets—Updated!* by David Lynn. Permission to reproduce this page granted only for use in the buyer's own youth group. www.YouthSpecialties.com

67

LIAR, LIAR [h o n e s t y]

THIS WEEK

It's easy to get away with being dishonest these days. One can easily fake it in an online chat room, shoplift small items at the store, or fib to parents. But dishonesty is more than just telling lies. As young people get older, they start to wrestle with honesty as a value. They must decide whether or not to be a completely honest person.

OPENER

How well does your group know each other? Try playing Two Truths and a Lie. Have the kids write three statements about themselves, two of which are true and one of which is not. If the kids choose two truths that sound like lies and a lie that sounds good, they'll be able to fool the group. The group must try to guess which one of the three is a lie.

Another idea is to conduct a lying contest. Have a contest to find out who can tell the biggest lie. After each student has told his fib, vote on the best tall tale. Give a prize to the winner, or simply announce you'll give $100 to the winner—then later admit that you lied!

THE DISCUSSION, BY THE NUMBERS

1. The main issue here is trust. Who do they trust to tell the truth? If there are those on the list that the group thinks is dishonest, ask them why. It will probably be due to a past experience with dishonesty. Trust takes time to develop and they destroy it when they are dishonest with each other.

2. Allow enough time for the group to share and discuss their opinions. You may want to discuss "white" and "black" lies, asking the kids to give examples of each and why they feel they are permissible lies or not. You may want to discuss the kind of lies that are considered "good"— such as telling someone they look nice when they don't or lying to protect a friend from harm. Is this right or wrong?

3. Ask the kids to share their rankings and to give reasons for their choices. There may be considerable difference of opinion here, so allow time for debate.

4. This attention-getter will give you a real-life situation to discuss with the kids. Ask them to decide what Natalie should have done and what she should do now. Ask them to consider all the possible consequences of this kind of dishonesty. Even though Natalie got away with it, there is no way of knowing what might happen as a result.

On the other hand, everyone knows the result of being completely honest.

5. These verses examine different aspects of honesty. Discuss each one as you study what God has to say about honesty.

THE CLOSE

You maybe want to focus some of your closing remarks on the consequences of honesty and dishonesty. How can dishonesty blow up in your face? Help your group understand that one lie tends to lead to another. And being known as a dishonest person can ruin your reputation and your sense of self-worth. One of the key characteristics of a Christian is honesty and being trustworthy. How can they imitate Christ? By being truthful and honest as he was. Remind them that God will forgive and forget them for past lies.

MORE

● Challenge your kids to ask their parents for a story of when they weren't completely truthful as teenagers, and what happened as a result. Parents often have some funny (or not so funny) stories to share. Have your kids get one honesty tip from their parents to bring next time and compile those for all to see.

● On a whiteboard or poster board, have your kids list character traits of a dishonest and honest person. How can they tell if someone is being dishonest? What traits of honesty are the most important? How does one's credibility affect how others see them?

● While they are watching TV, listening to the radio, reading magazines, and surfing the Internet this week, have your kids look for dishonesty in the media. How does the media use dishonesty to sell products, make money, or lie to the public? In what ways is the media dishonest? Are there specific TV shows, advertised brands, or Web sites that are not credible?

PROBLEMS PLUS

1. What do you think are the most common problems of people your age? Check three.
   ___ getting bad grades
   ___ having health problems
   ___ having no friends
   ___ being bored
   ___ feeling spiritually down
   ___ having strict parents
   ___ being hooked on drugs or alcohol
   ___ having a bad self-esteem
   ___ being pressured to have sex
   ___ worrying about family problems
   ___ not having a boyfriend or girlfriend

2. Finish this statement.
   If I could change one thing about my life, it would be—

3. Which of these is true for you? Compared to most people my age, I have—
   ❑ **more problems.**
   ❑ **less problems.**
   ❑ **about the same number of problems.**

4. How serious are each of the following problems in your life? Then, answer with **G (grande)** or **P (pequeño)**. (Spanish, silly! Big or small.)
   ___ a. I feel lonely most of the time.
   ___ b. I feel far away from God.
   ___ c. My parents don't understand me.
   ___ d. I feel depressed a lot of the time.
   ___ e. Church is boring.
   ___ f. I don't feel good about myself.
   ___ g. My teachers don't like me.
   ___ h. I get myself in trouble a lot of the time.
   ___ i. I have some bad habits.

5. What do you think each verse has to say about problems?

   Psalm 18:32   2 Corinthians 1:3-5

   Mark 4:39-40   1 Thessalonians 5:18

PROBLEMS PLUS [adolescent problems]

THIS WEEK

Each stage of life presents its own unique set of problems. Early adolescence is no exception. Most young people at this stage of life lack the experience and resources that adults have in dealing with problems. Some teenagers don't know who to go to with certain problems or how to solve them. This TalkSheet will give you an opportunity to talk about common problems, concerns, and frustrations of the junior high and middle school years, and how to solve them.

OPENER

What problems are junior highers or middle schoolers dealing with? On pieces of paper, have your kids write down problems that they or their peers face. Collect their answers and then read each on aloud. Give the group time to brainstorm ways that each problem could be solved. How do males handle problems differently from females? Do teens and adults face problems the same way? Why or why not? How might different people deal with a specific problem?

You may want to list the solutions on a whiteboard or poster board and talk about the different ways to deal with a problem (i.e. confronting a person versus talking behind the person's back). Also discuss healthy ways to deal with problems (i.e. letting your anger cool off versus hitting your brother).

THE DISCUSSION, BY THE NUMBERS

1. Go through this list and ask for a show of hands on each of the problems. Decide which one is the biggest. Are there problems common to their peers that aren't listed? Include some discussion about these problems, too.

2. Make a master list of all the changes your kids would like. Talk about what ones they have control over and the ones they don't. Ask them why they want to make these changes.

3. How would they answer for teenagers who may be minorities? Disabled? Live in a third world country? Have a AIDS or cancer? Your group may soon see their own problems in a different light.

4. Brainstorm a solution for each of these problems. This will give your kids some good practice in problem solving. You may also wish to go back to question 1 and discuss solutions to the problems identified there.

5. These passages look at problems from different perspectives. Ask several kids to read what they have written. What do your kids currently do to deal with problems? Do they think God cares about their problems? Can God solve all their problems?

THE CLOSE

Bible characters faced problems of all kinds—on example is the story of David and Goliath. Goliath presented an enormous (and very tall!) problem for David. Communicate with your kids that the biggest problems are chances to grow. That's God's way of making us stronger and more solid in our faith.

Reassure your kids that everyone has problems. As the leader, be careful that you don't gloss over these problems. Be aware that some of your group members may be dealing with some larger, more complicated problems, though—maybe an abusive parent, an eating disorder, or depression. If they don't want to or can't talk to a parent, encourage them to find another trustworthy adult like yourself, the pastor, school counselor—or you.

Most important, remind them that God is waiting to listen. Encourage them to take their problems to him. His arms are open wide, waiting to take them in and give them his peace.

MORE

● Have your kids think of the biggest problem that they are facing at the moment. Have them write this problem—along with their birthday instead of their name—and explain the problem on the top half of a piece of 8½ x 11 paper. Then pass out the problem papers to some mature senior highers, parents, or other adults for them to write down some thoughts, advice, or favorite verse that would help deal with the problem. Then return these papers to the junior highers (using their birthdays). Was the advice helpful? What kind of advice was given? Communicate that people who are older have experienced some of the same problems they do, and encourage your youth to seek out adults for advice and encouragement.

● Consider setting up up an e-mail or snail mail support network for your kids. Encourage them to send e-mail or mail to you with prayer requests or concerns that they'd like others to pray for. Distribute this list to your group once a week or so. Emphasize the importance of supporting each other through prayer, as well as praying for your own struggles.

YOUTH GROUP SCOOP

1. What is the **best** thing about this youth group?

2. Circle one of the words listed below that best describes this youth group.

struggling	dead	boring
loving	fun	growing
social	alive	average
friendly	great	judgmental

3. If you could change **one thing** about this youth group to make it better, what would you change?

4. After each sentence, please write **yes** or **no** and one reason why.

   a. Our youth group has good leaders.

   b. I feel like I'm an integral part of this youth group.

   c. I attend youth group meetings mainly because my parents make me.

   d. This youth group is important to me.

   e. I feel close to God because of this youth group.

   f. I have a lot of good friends in this youth group.

   g. What they do in youth group helps me.

   h. I feel like I can invite my friends to this youth group.

5. Read **Ephesians 4:1-6**, then write a short paragraph explaining what you've learned and how it can improve the youth group. Use the back of this sheet if you need to.

YOUTH GROUP SCOOP [youth group evaluation]

THIS WEEK

Young people often take their youth group for granted. When they're having fun and it's going great, they enjoy it. But when there is heavy discussion or less exciting activities, they complain. This session gives you and your group the opportunity to assess the status of the group in a positive way. You can also use this TalkSheet with the leaders of the group as a planning tool.

OPENER

There are a few different ways to approach this topic with your youth group. No matter what, try to stay positive about the group—don't let this turn into a gripe session. Encourage your kids to talk about other groups they've visited or been part of. Have them share the pros and cons of the activities, leaders, Bible studies, and so on. Jumpstart them with questions like—what did you like about the last group you were a part of? What did you like about the activities? Were you able to talk with the leaders? What made you frustrated? What made you want to go back?

Or ask your kids to list characteristics and features of a perfect youth group. Write the comments on a poster board or whiteboard so that you can look at them later. Then communicate that no group can be perfect because its members are so different! Each person in the group likes to do different things, which is why it's hard for leaders to please everyone.

THE DISCUSSION, BY THE NUMBERS

1. Begin by setting the tone and stating that you want to keep the discussion positive. Be sure to note any negative comments that come out, but mediate the discussion.

2. What words did they circle? Why did they choose the ones they did? Why didn't they choose the ones they didn't? Ask them to list any additional words that describe the youth group.

3. Let the kids to share their criticisms in a constructive way. Remind them the purpose of this is to improve the group, not bring it down.

4. Keep this exercise as positive as possible. Ask for volunteers to share their responses to the questions one at a time, or to make comments.

5. Have the kids share ways they feel the group could improve. Encourage them to write their comments down. You may want to collect these TalkSheets to read later and get a better idea of how they feel. Tell them in advance not to write their names on the TalkSheet.

THE CLOSE

If you'd like to do a closing activity, try the affirmation circle. Most teenagers don't hear enough good things about themselves, especially from their peers. It works like this—have everyone sit in a circle with one person in the middle. Those sitting in the circle give compliments to the person in the middle. Don't force them, though—you may have to start them up with a few questions beforehand like—

* what has this person meant to you?
* what does he or she add to the group?
* what are you thankful for about this person?
* does he or she have personality characteristics that you admire? If so, what?
* has this person taught you anything about God?

This can be a humbling experience, especially for those who aren't used to hearing compliments. Be sure to include your adult leaders and all your group members and do be sensitive to everyone in your group. It'll probably be easier for group members to find compliments for the more popular, outgoing kids. Be careful not to let the group go overboard on one person! This activity may be harder for the more quiet, withdrawn kids in your group.

Finally, let the group know that they are important to the group and that their comments and concerns will be taken seriously. You may want to invite them to get involved in the group activities—possibly help with planning and organizing meetings and events. Then close with an prayer for the youth group and its leaders.

MORE

● Invite your kids who are interested to a planning session to help brainstorm ideas for activities and programs for the coming year. This can be fun time of reflection and listening to suggestions. Maybe host a special breakfast or dessert night to do this. Encourage them to continue to let you know what they'd like to see happen in the group.

● Have some one-on-one time with your kids who are leaving the group and moving up to senior high. Ask him or her specific questions about what they liked about the year's activities. What new things did they learn? What was their favorite activity? Their favorite discussion? What wouldn't they want to do again? This is a great way to touch base with individual kids and hear their opinions in private.

SO WHO YOU LOOKIN' AT?

1. Compared to others your age, when it comes to the categories below how would you rate yourself on a scale of 1-10 (5 being average)?

Your looks—	1	2	3	4	5	6	7	8	9	10
Your intellect—	1	2	3	4	5	6	7	8	9	10
Your personality—	1	2	3	4	5	6	7	8	9	10
Your popularity—	1	2	3	4	5	6	7	8	9	10

2. What are some things about **yourself** that you are proud of?

3. Is this you or not? Answer **me** or **not me**.
   _____ a. I like the way I look.
   _____ b. I live my life the way I think others want me to live it.
   _____ c. Sometimes I wish I were someone else.
   _____ d. I don't think I am normal.
   _____ e. I sometimes do things I know I shouldn't, in order to be accepted.
   _____ f. I believe God loves me just the way I am.
   _____ g. When I meet new people, I worry they may not like me the way I am.

4. The following is a paraphrase of **Psalm 139:13-18**. Write your name in the blanks and then read it to yourself.

   God, you created all the complex parts of my body, while I was still inside my mother. Thank you, Lord, for creating me, _____ [your name]. I know you cared when you made me. While my bones were still forming, before anyone else knew who I was, you knew I, _____ [your name], was alive. You could see who I was even before I was born, and you had already planned my days on earth before I lived any one of them. You think about me all the time. You love me so much. Every minute, even when I get up in the morning, you are thinking about me.

   What **does** God think of you?

SO WHO YOU LOOKIN' AT? [self-image and self-esteem]

THIS WEEK

Self-esteem is a huge concern among teenage boys and girls. They feel so much pressure to fit in and they worry about their looks, how they act, and if they'll be accepted and liked by their peers. This TalkSheet gives your group the opportunity to discuss self-image and self-esteem and will give you a chance to affirm your kids.

OPENER

Everyone needs to hear affirmations, so have your group give each other a pat on the back—but not literally. Ask each person to trace his or her hand with a marker on a piece of 81/2 x 11 paper. Then have them tape the papers on each other's backs. Make sure each group member has a pen, pencil, or marker to write with. Then, encourage them to walk around and write something they like about the person in the hand. Ask your kids to think of a less superficial comment—maybe something about personality or talents. Give the group enough time to write on each person's back. Then let the kids read their own papers and share how this activity made them feel.

THE DISCUSSION, BY THE NUMBERS

1. Don't ask the kids to share their personal answers. Instead, have them think about their answers and what they've learned about themselves. A person's self-image is usually based on how they think others feel about them.

   Communicate that a good self-image comes from accepting and respecting yourself—not from what others think about you.

2. Ask the kids to share the traits they are proud of. Or have them share what they would be proud of if they were the person on their right. Keep the focus on personal qualities and accomplishments.

3. You may want to make this a general discussion—focus on a how a teenage girl or guy may feel. Your kids may open up more freely if you share how you felt about yourself when you were a teenager.

4. This passage has been paraphrased to emphasize the fact that God loves each person for who they are. Have the group read the verses aloud and then lead a discussion about how these verses apply to feelings of self-esteem. How does God feel when they don't like ourselves?

THE CLOSE

Communicate clearly that everyone—even those who look like they have it all together—struggle with self-image. Even adults still feel badly about themselves from time to time. Challenge your kids to begin seeing themselves as God sees them—as children he loves. In fact, God commands us to love ourselves as we love others (Leviticus 19:18).

Emphasize to your kids that God has created each of them with potential—and he will use them if they give their lives to him. There are several biblical characters who struggled with self-worth, including Moses (who had a speech impediment) and Paul (who apparently wasn't very handsome and had a "thorn in the flesh"). If they keep putting themselves down, God can't use them to their fullest and best.

Point out that it's hard to keep a positive self-image when the media tells us otherwise. TV, radio, movies, advertisements tell us how to act, look, dress, what products to use, how be popular, and who to hang out with. They are constantly bombarded with messages that tell us they aren't good enough. But they have control over it—they can keep things in perspective with God's help.

MORE

● You may want to go a bit further to encourage your kids by sending each one an encouraging postcard, note, or e-mail during the week. Point out specific reasons why you appreciate about them and what makes them special.

● What do your kids think about themselves? Ask your kids write a letter to themselves in a self-addressed stamped envelope. Encourage them to write down how they feel about themselves, what they struggle with, and what they'd like to change. Challenge them to set goals for themselves of what they'd like to work on to improve their self-images. Send these letters to your kids after a couple of months. How are they doing? What changes have they made?

● Or check out what the media says about self-image. On a poster board or whiteboard, ask the group to list specific attitudes and messages that the media sends about self-respect and self-esteem. What pressures to your kids feel from the media and others? How do these pressures affect their self-image and that of other teens? How can they resist what TV, radio, the Internet, and movies are telling them?

GO FOR IT!

1. Name **one person** who you think is successful.

2. Rate the people described below from **most successful (1)** to **least successful (7)**.
   ___ Someone who gets all A's
   ___ Someone who is popular in school
   ___ Someone who always tells her parents the truth
   ___ Someone who volunteers to help in the church nursery
   ___ Someone who is outstanding in sports
   ___ Someone who has lots of friends
   ___ Someone who goes to church every week

3. If you had to give up **three** things from those listed below, which would they be?

computer	**best friend(s)**
TV	**parents**
health	**freedom**
faith	**allowance**

4. Answer each of the following questions by **circling one** of the choices.

   a. How important is **being popular** to you?
      Really important
      Kind of important
      A wee bit important
      Not really important

   b. How important is **money** to you?
      Really important
      Kind of important
      A wee bit important
      Not really important

   c. **Who** is the most successful?
      Millionaire
      Professional athlete
      Music legend
      Teacher
      Missionary

   d. **What** would you rather be?
      Smart
      Powerful
      Rich
      Healthy

   e. What kind of **life** do you want?
      Exciting
      Spiritual
      Comfortable
      Fulfilling

   f. **How** do you want others to see you as?
      Extraordinary
      Important
      Average
      Special

5. Read each of the Bible verses and finish the sentences accordingly.
   Matthew 10:39
      The world says focus on yourself, but the Bible says—

   John 15:18-21
      The world says it loves you, but the Bible says—

   1 John 2:15-17
      The world says it has a lot to offer you, but the Bible says—

GO FOR IT! [success]

THIS WEEK

Think about it—our society is success-obsessed! We are flooded with different messages about how to look better, make more money, and be more popular. The media tells us that success means having money, prestige, and power. Our young people are convinced that they must have the best clothes, the right friends, and hang with the in-crowd. This TalkSheet will help you talk about success and what it means for Christians.

OPENER

Your kids may have different ideas about what success is. So in your intro, have them make a list of characteristics of success—what do peers their age need to be successful? Be sure to distinguish between being popular and successful. Use a whiteboard or poster board to keep track of these. Some suggestions may include things like having cool friends, wearing the right clothes, having a boyfriend or girlfriend, and getting good grades. Compare the items on this list and circle the ones are the most important. Discuss which of the items are character traits (such as being friendly and courteous) and which ones are superficial (such as good looks and nice clothes).

THE DISCUSSION, BY THE NUMBERS

1. Have the kids share the names they chose. Why did they chose them? Then, have them take a vote for the most successful person alive today. How about a person not alive? This will give you a good idea of who your kids consider successful.

2. This activity focuses on the priorities that your kids have. Have them choose what activity is more successful and then share their rankings. If there are lots of opinions, ask them to share their thoughts. How would God view these priorities?

3. Most young people don't think about giving things up. This will get them thinking about what's truly important to them and what isn't. Feel free to add to this list.

4. Have the group share their choices and share why they chose them. Be careful not to focus on specific individuals. Encourage them to share how they think teenagers in general would answer. Discuss the different opinions and how these affect our lives as Christians.

5. This activity contrasts secular philosophy with a biblical one. Take some time to make a second list (from the opener) of what makes a person successful in God's eyes. Compare these two lists. How do the lists differ? What items stand out on each list? How does the world's view of success differ from that of God's?

THE CLOSE

Communicate with your kids that everyone is successful in different ways. Some people do better in school while some others have more friends. God has given people different gifts and abilities that lead to success. But even the most successful people—including very famous, rich celebrities—can feel empty and unfulfilled.

The Bible asks, "What does it profit a man if he should gain the whole world and lose his soul?" (Matthew 16:26). Worldly success doesn't last forever. God wants us to seek him and his will first—then he'll bless us with success. Where is your heart? Are you caught up in worldly success or spiritual success?

MORE

- You may want to use this time to explain what goals are, why they are important, and how to set them. Also, encourage them to think BIG! Having goals and dreams is important for understanding who they are and what they are capable of. Ask each of your kids to make a list of at least three things that they'd like to do within the next five years. Then, another list of 10 things they'd like to do over their lifetime. You also have the option of letting them do this letter-style and send you the letters to them back to them in a few months.

- Need a more visual activity? Ask the group to cut pictures out of magazines that portray success according to the media and our society. These may include pictures of actors or actresses, athletes, politicians, or pictures of successful family members or other acquaintances. They may include words that describe or determine success as well. Use this collage to talk about how the media and society views success. What negative messages does it give? What positive messages are there? How does this representation of success compare with that of God's view of success?

CAN YOU BUY THAT?

1. Think of your favorite **television commercial**. What product does it advertise?

2. When you make a purchase, do you usually buy the **advertised brand** (the one you recognize) or **another one** (say "Brand X")? Give one example of each.
   ❑ **Advertised brand—**   ❑ **Brand X—**

3. List **one brand name** for the products below. Can you remember the advertisement for it?

   Makeup—   Soft drink—
   Perfume or cologne—   Shampoo—
   Video games—   Car—
   Cereal—   Toothpaste—
   Beer—   Clothing—
   Shoes—   Pizza—

4. Do you **A (agree)** or **D (disagree)**?
   ___ a. Commercials are good because they help people decide what to buy.
   ___ b. People buy many things they don't need because of advertising.
   ___ c. People would be better off without advertising.
   ___ d. Celebrities shouldn't make commercials.
   ___ e. Most commercials are truthful.
   ___ f. Advertisers shouldn't use sex to sell their products.

5. What do the following Bible verses have to say about **advertising**?

   Ephesians 4:17-19

   Ephesians 5:6

   1 John 3:7-8

CAN YOU BUY THAT? [advertising]

THIS WEEK

Our society is engulfed by advertising. Think about it—it's everywhere! It's on TV, radio, billboards, stadium scoreboards, racecars, blimps, and airplanes—even on clothing! Companies target young people to create loyalty to a brand. And since teenagers are the age group that spends the most money on CDs, clothes, and movies, they're prime targets. But, they're a bit naïve about what they see and hear. This discussion allows you to point out how false advertising can trick them into the "gotta have it" mentality.

OPENER

Videotape several TV commercials and show them to your group. After each one, stop and talk about the ad. What did the advertisement say? What makes you want (or not to!) buy the product? What is manipulative about the ad, if anything?

Explain that companies spend millions of dollars in advertising every year. On a given Super Bowl Sunday, companies spend millions for every second of airtime. Why do they put so much money and energy into advertising? What are some of the best advertisements that your kids have seen? Why did they like them?

Another good lead-in is to make a list of advertising slogans and have the kids guess the product each represents. You'll be amazed what they remember and recognize! Feel free to use this as a game and give points to teams who can name the most slogans in a given amount of time.

THE DISCUSSION, BY THE NUMBERS

1. Let the kids share their favorite commercials. Why do they like them? Have they bought the product? Why or why not?

2. Most will respond by saying, "It depends..." A good way to handle this is to make two lists, one of advertised brands and another Brand X. Then write the reasons given for each answer.

3. See how many different brand names your group can think of for each product. Discuss how they became aware of the brand. Point out how easy it is to remember certain ads—the mark of an effective advertisement!

4. This will most likely create a variety of responses. Let your kids debate the different issues. You might wish to have them take sides for their positions in a debate-style of discussion. Try to cover as many points of view as possible and keep the discussion open-minded.

5. Ask for their opinions—how can they apply these Bible verses to their lives? What do these say about today's advertising? How does this change how they view advertising?

THE CLOSE

Challenge your kids to take a close look at the ads they watch and hear. Since the goal is to make money, advertisers will always try to make the product look good. Talk about ways that they can discern these messages. What questions can they ask when they see or hear an ad? How can they limit the amount of ads that they see or hear?

Point out that advertising isn't all bad. In fact, there are benefits to learning about a product. But, ads can also deceive and lie. What messages do your kids see or remember that aren't true?

Communicate how God views money and advertising. Getting caught up in the "gotta have it" mentality is unhealthy and sinful. Help your kids see that with that attitude they'll start to want more and more—soon they become more greedy and unhappy with what they have. God wants us to be content and to rely on him. How does advertising affect the way they view God? Can it affect our relationship with him? How?

MORE

● Just how surrounded are your kids by advertisements? Ask your group to keep a list of everywhere they see advertisements. They might not realize just how surrounded they are by ads. Challenge them to take a close look during the week as they go to school and hang out with friends. Have them keep an eye out for ads on clothing, on buses, on the Internet, and even on cereal boxes. Have them bring their lists and talk about them. Where did they see advertising? How did it make them feel?

● What impact has advertising had on national holidays, especially Christmas? Talk about advertising in this context. How would they view Christmas if they didn't have to shop, buy, or receive gifts? What if there were no Easter bunnies or gifts from Santa? What if Valentine's Day was just about showing love and not giving away roses, candy, or paper cards? What meaning (both religious and not) has the media and society given our holidays, like Easter or Thanksgiving? Make a two-column list—With ads and Without ads. Have them list words or ideas about each holiday from these perspectives. Holidays to include in the discussion are Easter, Christmas, All Saints Day (Halloween), Thanksgiving, and the Fourth of July.

I WONDER

1. What do you sometimes **wonder** about?
   - ❑ If God exists
   - ❑ If the devil exists
   - ❑ If there really is a heaven
   - ❑ If God answers my prayers
   - ❑ If the theory of evolution is true
   - ❑ If the Bible is true
   - ❑ If Jesus actually rose from the dead
   - ❑ If there are angels
   - ❑ If hell is really fiery
   - ❑ If Jesus is God and vice versa

2. If a people have doubts and questions about God, what should they do?
   - ❑ Ignore their doubts
   - ❑ Stop doubting and trust God
   - ❑ Get a cheeseburger
   - ❑ Repent
   - ❑ Look on the Internet
   - ❑ Ask someone about them
   - ❑ Pray
   - ❑ Turn to Buddhism
   - ❑ Ask God directly
   - ❑ Read their Bible

3. Mark these statements **true** or **false**—
   Doubts about God are normal. _____
   When I doubt God, he's angry. _____
   Men and women of the Bible never doubted God. _____
   God understands and accepts my doubts. _____
   If a person has doubts, then he has no faith. _____

4. Read the following Bible passages and summarize them in **five words or less.**

   Psalm 10:1—

   John 20:29—

   Hebrews 11:6—

I WONDER [d o u b t]

THIS WEEK

It's normal and healthy for teenagers to doubt and question what they believe. Most of them are searching to find who they are and what they believe. They're looking for answers and dealing with tough questions. It's important for them to be able to discuss these doubts and questions with an adult like their youth leader. This session isn't able to answer all their questions and doubts, but will help them understand that having doubts is normal, even among adults.

OPENER

Make them wonder! Make a list of the top 10 biggest mysteries or doubts that your kids have—things that your group wonders about. Discuss possible solutions or answers for each one. How will they find the answers, if they can? What baffles them so about these mysteries or doubts? Some of these may include questions about how God made the world from nothing, how Jesus was God and man, whether they'll ever travel to Mars, et cetera. You never know what doubts or mysteries your kids will come up with!

Ask your group to role-play situations in which they must defend their beliefs. Split them up into groups and have one group play the devil's advocates. One group must defend their side and their beliefs—not only their faith in God, but other issues, like how God created the earth or why there is a heaven and hell. Challenge them to use their Bibles to defend what they are saying. This can be an incredible way to get your kids thinking (depending on your group, of course!)

THE DISCUSSION, BY THE NUMBERS

1. Some kids won't admit their doubts in any of these areas. Go down the list and ask if any have wondered about each one. If they express no doubts, pressure them a little. For example, say something like, "Since you're so sure about this one, maybe you can help me. Tell me what makes you so certain." If they're being honest, they'll admit to having serious doubts about most of these issues.

2. The purpose of this is to encourage the kids to talk about their doubts and questions. Let them know you are always available to listen to the questions they might have.

3. Use this to communicate that doubt is normal for all of us. Reinforce the idea that God won't ever reject us—not even for doubting. When the kids begin to share some of their doubts, don't feel pressured give all the answers. Sometimes adults don't know everything!

Point out that doubt strengthens our faith. If you're absolutely certain about something then there's no need for faith. Faith is believing even when you doubt.

4. Let the group share their summaries. Ask them if they think God understands their doubts. How does God feel about us doubting him? How can doubt get in the way of our faith?

THE CLOSE

Tell the story of John the Baptist—how he confidently announced the coming of Christ and then, when he was thrown into prison, began to have doubts about whether or not Jesus was really who he was (Luke 7:18-23).

Reiterate the fact that doubts are normal and are necessary for stretching our faith and beliefs. Wondering and doubting doesn't meet that they don't have faith—it isn't a sin. But it does weaken our faith in God, who is in complete control. Challenge your kids to stretch their minds and their faith. Encourage them to bring their questions to parents, teachers, or you—people who care about them and may be able to help them figure out some answers.

MORE

● Several biblical characters had serious doubts about what God was doing. A few of them were major characters like Moses, Abraham, Peter, and Thomas. Ask your group to find examples of doubting characters in the Bible and let them share their findings. Who had doubts? What were the doubts? Are these still concerns that they have today? How did God address the situation? What happened after they understood?

● Challenge your kids to think about trust in light of doubting. What is trust? How does trusting compare to having faith? Do your kids trust only those things that they see? For example, how easy is it to trust God? Would they trust God more if they could see or touch him? How can your kids strengthen their faith in God? How does trusting others affect trust in God? Is it easier to trust people or God?

OH, GOD

1. **Circle** the words that you think best describe what God is like.

holy	mysterious	eternal
loving	motherly	nonexistent
strict	fatherly	weak
smart	out of it	unfair
American	just	grandfatherly
freak	merciful	uncaring
powerful	creative	mean
dead	patient	gracious

2. If you could ask God one question, what would it be?

3. If God wrote you an e-mail, what do you think he'd say to you?

4. Dionte has always believed in God, but he's never felt really close to God or felt that God actually cared about him. What would you tell Dionte about getting to know God better?

5. Look up the following passages and decide which ones **describe God** and which ones don't.

Deuteronomy 32:4	John 4:24
Psalm 118:29	Romans 11:33
Matthew 6:33	Romans 12:1
Matthew 7:11	

OH, GOD [God]

THIS WEEK

How familiar are you with your kids' beliefs? Do you know about their reasons for believing in God? This discussion will allow you to talk about what your student believe—what they think God is like and how their belief in God makes a difference in their lives. You'll want to make sure that your group members are comfortable with each other before you tackle this discussion. Sometimes it's not easy for them to open up about their beliefs, so be sure to provide a warm environment where they feel supported.

OPENER

You can introduce this in many different ways, depending on the size and maturity of your group. You may want to have them list phrases or words that describe God. You can play a reverse-Pictionary type game with this as well. Have them list their words that describe God. Then, have group members take turns drawing the descriptive words while the other group members guess the words. It's challenging, but it gets them thinking.

Or share a story with them about God. Have your kids act out the parable of the lost son (Luke 15:11-27) while you read the story, either from the Bible or another version of the story. How does the parable describe God? What characteristics does God have from the parable? How about the parable of the lost sheep (Luke 15:3-7)?

THE DISCUSSION, BY THE NUMBERS

1. Have the kids share the words they chose and think of additional words to describe God. Ask them why they chose certain words.

2. Let the kids share their questions and try to answer them as a group. Some simply won't have answers—that's okay. Help them understand that God has answers to our questions, even though they don't always know what they are.

3. Ask several kids to share their e-mails. Did this help them understand God better? What did they learn about God? Emphasize that God has already written us a letter—the Bible. In it, he tells us stories and gives us advice on all kinds of stuff. Challenge your kids to dig in and start getting to know God better.

4. Use this tension-getter to discuss practical ways to have a better relationship with God. Make a master list of all the suggestions that the group gives. You may want to add some of your own. Challenge your kids to pick one and do it for a week.

5. What did these verses say? How do these verses relate to what they've learned about God?

THE CLOSE

God thinks so much of all his children. You may want to read a verse or two to the group that describes how much God loves them. Point out that they each are the jewel of God's eye. If he had a computer, their picture would be on the screensaver. He hangs out with them all the time—how often to they hang out with him? If they could chat with God on the phone, what would they say?

Close with a time of prayer. If your junior high and middle school kids aren't comfortable praying aloud, ask them to write a short prayer on the back of their TalkSheet. Then give them some time for silent prayer.

MORE

- It's important to set goals for getting to know God better. Challenge them to do more than just pray and read the Bible—to set specific goals, like praying for ten minutes everyday, reading a chapter from the Bible every other day, or meeting with you and a small group every couple weeks. Encourage them set these realistic goals and write them on a 3x5 card to keep. Remind them that they can come to you with struggles or questions that they may have—everyone needs to be encouraged spiritually.

- Set up an e-mail resource for encouraging prayer and Scripture reading. Have your kids e-mail each other or you their favorite verses, new things they've learned, or prayer requests they have. Challenge them to encourage each other to learn more about God. Collect and distribute the e-mails once (or more) a week.

JUST TRUST ME

1. **Circle** those from this list that you could trust—

the President	your father
your mom	your youth pastor
a door-to-door salesman	a police officer
God	yourself
your brother or sister	a stranger
a school teacher	a music star
a famous TV actor or actress	your boyfriend or girlfriend

2. **Check** the most honest answer.

My parents can trust me—
- ❏ a. all of the time.
- ❏ b. some of the time.
- ❏ c. never.

My teachers can trust me—
- ❏ a. all of the time.
- ❏ b. some of the time.
- ❏ c. never.

My friends can trust me—
- ❏ a. all of the time.
- ❏ b. some of the time.
- ❏ c. never.

3. Was there a time when a person **trusted** you with a lot?

What happened and why?

What made you trustworthy?

4. Write **agree** or **disagree** for each of these statements.

_____ a. The average person can usually be trusted.

_____ b. It's better to trust Christians than non-Christians.

_____ c. It's difficult to know who to trust these days.

_____ d. Once a person lies to you or doesn't keep a promise, it's impossible to trust that person again.

_____ e. It's best not to trust anyone.

5. Rewrite **Proverbs 3:5-6** in your own words.

JUST TRUST ME [trust]

THIS WEEK

Trust is a big issue in the lives of kids today. Some don't trust their parents or the adults in their lives. Some have been hurt and abused. Others don't have many friends and don't trust other people with their feelings and emotions. It's important to teach them what trust is and what it means for Christians. This TalkSheet will direct your discussion on believing in others and how God fits into this picture.

OPENER

Start by holding an envelope in your hand. In this envelope is a blank piece of paper and a small prize—either a dollar bill (or more), a gift certificate, or a coupon for a free dessert. Ask your group who would like an envelope—but don't tell them. Remind them that they don't know what's in the envelope! Are they willing to risk taking the envelope without knowing what's in it? What makes them trust you or not trust you? Are they going to take the envelope without knowing what the consequences are?

Finally, if someone does take the envelope, stop before handing over the envelope. Ask them in front of the others why they want the envelope and why they trust you. Then hand over the envelope and let them open it. Of course, they won't have to do anything but take the prize!

If no one dares take the envelope, challenge them once more. Then, open the envelope and show them what was inside—a prize. They wouldn't have had to do anything but accept the prize!

THE DISCUSSION, BY THE NUMBERS

1. Ask the kids to share the words they circled. Ask why they think they can trust the people chosen. Have them pick out three people they consider to be the most untrustworthy. Why did they choose these people? What characteristics do untrustworthy people have?

2. This brings the trust issue closer to home. Some won't want to reveal their answers, so don't force them. Instead, ask them to think about why others may or may not trust them. What do they need to work on to be more trustworthy? Point out that trust is important for all good, healthy relationships.

3. Ask the kids to share any experiences here, if any. You can expand this question by asking if they can think of a time when a friend showed he or she could or couldn't be trusted or when a friend betrayed a trust. Remind them not to give specific names, though!

4. Take a poll on each of these issues and discuss each one. Ask the kids to explain why they feel a certain way. Be positive as you help them confront these statements. Help them see trust is necessary and important for good relationships and self-respect. If someone blows it, they need to be forgiven and rebuild that trust.

5. Have the kids share their sentences. Discuss how a person can trust God with their lives. Why is it sometimes hard not to trust God? How can they trust God in our daily lives? Communicate that God is trustworthy—all the time. He made us. He loves us. And, he knows what's best for us.

THE CLOSE

Communicate that some people can't be trusted. Other people seem like they can be trusted, when really they can't. Point out that they are deceived by other people, by the media and by ourselves. Trust takes time and patience. No one deserves to be instantly trusted. If someone breaks trust, it can take a long time—sometimes years—to be rebuilt. It's not easy to trust others and for others to trust us. Point out that your kids need to guard their hearts.

Your kids can ask God to heal them when they've been hurt. God forgives us even if people don't. You may want to take some time and talk about what breaks trust. If you sense that some of your kids are struggling with trusting others, they may be dealing with some larger issues, such as sexual abuse, problems at home, or having a hard time at school. If you sense an abusive situation, you must encourage the person to find help—and report it to the authorities in your area.

MORE

● On a whiteboard or poster board, write the word TRUST vertically. Split your group up into five smaller groups and give each group one letter of the word trust. Have each group list at least two words or phrases that describe trust and that start with the letter that they've been given. For example, if a group had T, they could list "telling the truth" or "trying to rely on another person." Then go over these with the group and discuss what the different phrases or words mean.

● How do TV shows and movies portray trust? Is it easy to trust the things they read in the newspapers or hear on the radio? How can they decide if something on the Internet is trustworthy or not? Why do they trust what advertisements say—even when they are false? See if your kids can share examples of how they've trusted—or not trusted—something they've seen or heard.

THIS MEANS WAR!

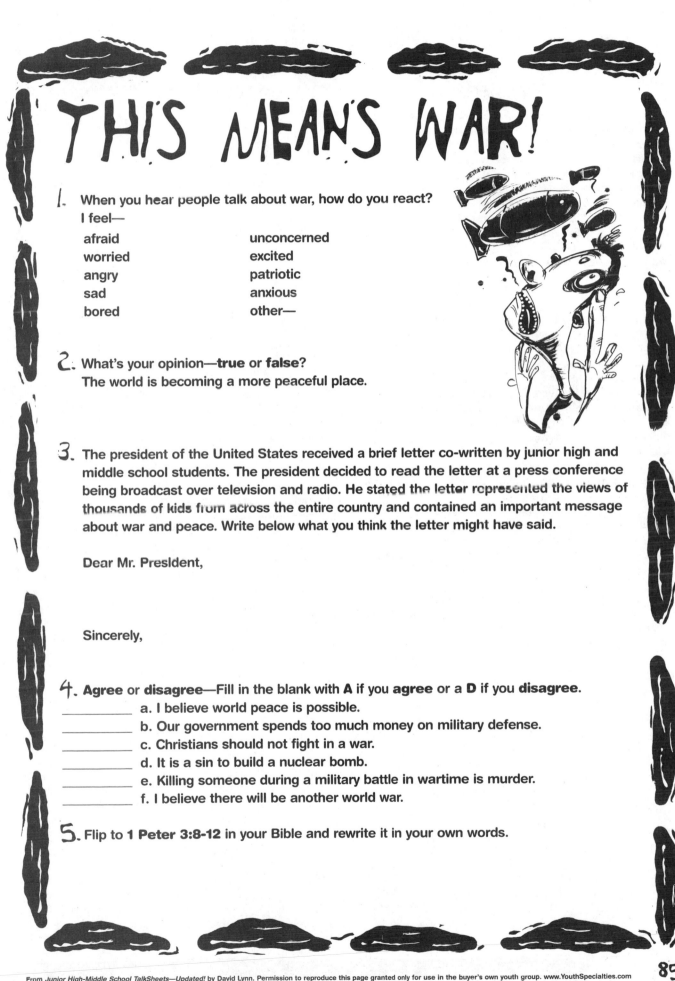

1. When you hear people talk about war, how do you react?
   I feel—

   afraid   unconcerned
   worried   excited
   angry   patriotic
   sad   anxious
   bored   other—

2. What's your opinion—**true** or **false**?
   The world is becoming a more peaceful place.

3. The president of the United States received a brief letter co-written by junior high and middle school students. The president decided to read the letter at a press conference being broadcast over television and radio. He stated the letter represented the views of thousands of kids from across the entire country and contained an important message about war and peace. Write below what you think the letter might have said.

   Dear Mr. President,

   Sincerely,

4. **Agree** or **disagree**—Fill in the blank with **A** if you **agree** or a **D** if you **disagree**.
   _____ a. I believe world peace is possible.
   _____ b. Our government spends too much money on military defense.
   _____ c. Christians should not fight in a war.
   _____ d. It is a sin to build a nuclear bomb.
   _____ e. Killing someone during a military battle in wartime is murder.
   _____ f. I believe there will be another world war.

5. Flip to **1 Peter 3:8-12** in your Bible and rewrite it in your own words.

THIS MEANS WAR! [w a r]

THIS WEEK

Unfortunately, kids live in a world full of war, and the news of these wars are brought home via television, newspapers, magazines, and the Internet. The threat of nuclear war is a real one. Junior high and middle school kids often see war portrayed in movies and on TV. This TalkSheet allows you to talk about this subject from a Christian perspective.

If you or your church takes a strong position on either side of the war and peace issue, you may use this discussion as a way to help your kids understand your view as well as to form one of their own.

OPENER

Split your group into smaller groups and give each one a situation to discuss. Encourage them to talk about the different options and the risks on all sides. Make a list of their ideas on a whiteboard or poster board.

Situation 1: There has been a report that the Chinese government has developed a biological weapon that destroys human flesh. It eats the flesh, killing people in agony—alive. If they were to drop the bomb, it would destroy an entire nation within three days. You are the President of the United States—you are enemies with the Chinese. How will you react after you are informed of this development? What would happen if the bomb leaked or accidentally was launched? What about the innocent people worldwide that could be affected by this?

Situation 2: You are a civilian living with your family in a large city in Italy. You've heard that some Turks are planning an attack on your government due to a bitter rivalry that has exploded. You fear for the lives of your children. But you don't have money to flee. Your city will most likely be hit by an air strike within 12 hours. How do you feel? What are you going to tell your children? What about your loved ones and friends in the same city? What do you think of the Turks now?

Situation 3: You are a high-ranking U.S. commander aboard a nuclear ship in the Indian Ocean. You've received word that the Russian government has a nuclear warhead aimed at the U.S. and is ready to launch. You must launch the nuclear weapon on your ship within 30 minutes. If you launch, 75 percent of Russia will be destroyed, killing millions of people. You don't know for sure if Russia has launched its weapon yet. If it has, over 50 percent of the United States has been destroyed, possibly wiping out your entire family. Will you launch? What effect could your command have on millions of people?

THE DISCUSSION, BY THE NUMBERS

1. If responses are slow on this, ask how they would feel in response to specific headlines, such as: "IRAQ THREATENS NUCLEAR ATTACK ON U.S.," Allow enough time for the kids to share their fears about the possibility of a nuclear or biological war.

2. Poll the kids to see how they voted and why.

3. Have several kids read their letters. Then see if they can come up with some concrete, specific ideas about how to prevent war.

4. Let the Agrees and the Disagrees debate. Provide input for them on items they are confused about. Keep in mind some of these issues are not directly addressed in the Bible, so there are many points of view, even among Christians.

5. Ask how these verses relate to war. Does it also relate to family fights? Disagreements with friends? Run-ins with your teammates or coach? Other verses to consider are James 4:1-2.

THE CLOSE

Communicate to your youth that war is brutal—it shouldn't be taken lightly. Although war is terrible, it is sometimes inevitable to keep world peace and protect our country. War is the price they pay for freedom and justice. As Christians they should support their country, but strive to be peacemakers. They should fight for and promote peace, acceptance, and love.

Don't leave this discussion in a negative light. Communicate that God is still in control of the world—he knows every person in every corner of the world. They don't have to be afraid.

MORE

● Show a clip of a movie that portrays war. Be sure to preview the clips before you show them. Suggestions include "Saving Private Ryan", "The Hunt for Red October", "Crimson Tide", "The Thin Red Line", or "Courage Under Fire". Why does government spend millions of dollars each year to prepare troops for war? How does that make your group feel? What scares them about war situations?

● Have your kids look in the Bible to find passages or stories of war. What do your kids think God's view of war is? What does your church say about war and peace?

BIG MOUTH

1. Read the statements and write whether you **agree** or **disagree**.

_____ a. There's too much dirty language on TV.

_____ b. Some swear words are okay, but others aren't.

_____ c. Most of my friends use bad language.

_____ d. Christians shouldn't ever swear or use dirty language.

_____ e. If a movie has bad language in the script, it should be boycotted.

_____ f. Swearing isn't such a big deal anymore; everybody does it.

_____ g. Words that don't use God's name are okay to say.

2. What does this verse say about our **language**?

   "But no man can tame the tongue. It is a restless evil, full of deadly poison" (James 3:8)

3. Coby swore at his best friend Jaydyn and said something pretty harsh. As the words left his mouth, he immediately wanted to take them back. If only he could've kept his mouth shut! Jaydyn stormed away with a pained look on his face. If you were Coby, what would you do now?

4. Which of these scenarios would you consider the **most hurtful**? Why?
   - ❑ Reaming out a sibling.
   - ❑ Making a snide comment to your mom.
   - ❑ Swearing after you stub your toe.
   - ❑ Teasing someone about their clothes.
   - ❑ Telling a teacher that you hate his or her class.
   - ❑ Laughing at someone's mistake.
   - ❑ Calling someone a loser.
   - ❑ Giving a friend the silent treatment.
   - ❑ Cussing out a teammate.
   - ❑ Making fun of someone's looks.

5. Read the following Bible verses, and complete the sentences in your own words.

   Proverbs 13:3—It is important to think before I speak, because—

   James 3:5—My mouth can get me into trouble, because—

   2 Timothy 2:16—I want to please God with the words from my mouth, because—

BIG MOUTH [taming the tongue]

THIS WEEK

Today our youth hear harsh gossip, abusive words, and vulgar language everywhere. In fact, most of your kids would consider this normal in our society. Certain words are built into our society's vocabulary—it's unavoidable to hear them in movies, on TV, on the radio, in songs, and in our schools. Unfortunately, your kids are able to list words that they hear used everyday—some that are shocking to hear used among middle schoolers. This TalkSheet will help you discuss the relationship between the Christian faith and the words that they speak.

OPENER

Pick a word that is commonly said among your group—not a swear word, just any word that they use a lot. All groups of kids have slang words or phrases that they use. Pick the word and write it on a whiteboard or a place where the kids can see it. If, during this TalkSheet, someone says the word or words that you chose, have your kids call each other on it. Decide a lighthearted (yet funny) consequence for using this word in the discussion—maybe getting squirted with a water gun or having someone hit a buzzer. Challenge your kids to pay close attention to how they speak and the words they choose. How many times did they call each other on this word? How hard was it for them to keep track of the things they said?

THE DISCUSSION, BY THE NUMBERS

1. This deals with swearing—which is common among youth. Where do they learn this language? Where do they pick up certain swear words? Besides hurting others, why is obscene language bad? What does God think about using these words? How do other see us when they use these words?

2. Our words are deadly and they can cause great pain to others. Like physical cuts, hurtful words take time to heal. Our tongue is a weapon—it can hurt others, cause problems, and even destroy relationships. God even warns us about it in the Bible.

3. Use this attention-getter to discuss practical ways to control one's tongue. Ask if anyone in the group has ever experienced anything similar. What are the consequences—both short and long term—of Coby's actions might be? How will their friendship change?

4. Have the kids share reasons. Decide as a group which one is the worst and why.

5. Ask the kids to read their sentences. How do these verses apply to their lives? What can they do as Christians when they are surrounded by negative language? How does loving God affect the way that they treat and speak to others?

THE CLOSE

The tongue is sharp and needs to be controlled—that's not always easy! Emphasize just how badly words hurt, how destructive they can be, and how they become used to what they hear around us. Challenge your kids to pay extra attention to what they see and hear this week. Like the game in the intro, they often don't even think about using certain words, including swear words.

Challenge your kids to hold each other and their friends and family members accountable for their language. If your kids struggle with using certain words, have them find a friend or parent that can call them on it. Have them set a personal goal of how they are going to change their language.

Finally, challenge your kids to find one person who they've hurt by their language and apologize for their hurtful words. Communicate how important it is to ask for forgiveness and heal our relationships with others. Take a few minutes to pray with your kids, asking for God's forgiveness and help to control our tongues.

MORE

● How often are swear words really used? Have the group check it out for themselves. Ask each of your kids to watch a TV show or movie—or listen closely to the lyrics in a CD—during the week and keep track of how many times swear words or vulgar language were used. Have them write down the words and how many times they were said. Compare the results the next week. What shows or movies had the most? How did the language fit in with what was going on in the story? What result did the language have, if any?

● What language are your kids hearing and using? Make a list of the most commonly used swear words and vulgar words that they hear used (if it won't offend anyone in your group or church too badly). You might be surprised what words you hear! There might be some you've never heard of. If you don't know what a word means, ask. On a whiteboard or poster board, have the group rank them from the least to most worst. Why are some of the words considered worse or more hurtful than the others? How can someone justify using some words more than others? How does God view some words as opposed to others? What would he say about using any of the words on the list?

I AIN'T GOT NOBODY

1. Name one of your closest friends.
   List three reasons why this person is a good friend.

2. Read the statements and react with **Y (Yes)**, **N (No)**, or **M (Maybe)**—

   _____ I would like to have more friends.
   _____ I think I can be a good friend to others.
   _____ I choose the right kind of friends.
   _____ A best friend should be a Christian.
   _____ Sometimes my friends are a bad influence on me.

   _____ I have a hard time making friends.
   _____ I wish I had a best friend.
   _____ I want to trade in the friends I have for some new ones.
   _____ My parents don't like my friends.
   _____ My friends talk about me behind my back.

3. Tyler is sitting alone in the cafeteria again. He's been at this new school for a month and still hasn't made any friends. He had one friend—or at least he thought that Micah was a friend. But Micah told all the guys the real reason that Tyler's family had to move was that Tyler's dad has AIDS and lost his job. Tyler had trusted Micah not to tell anyone. Now Tyler has decided to give up trying to make friends here again.

   Why did Micah tell the guys about Tyler's dad?

   How can Tyler make **new friends**?

   How can Tyler tell who his **true friends** are?

4. Read the following Bible verses and then complete the sentences.
   Job 2:11
   A friend is someone who—

   Ecclesiastes 4:10
   A friend is someone who—

I AIN'T GOT NOBODY [friendship]

THIS WEEK

Friendships are the heart and soul of the teenage years. There's hardly anything as important to junior high and middle school kids as having friends. Everyone wants to be accepted, fit in, and have fun with friends. There's no doubt that your kids will want to talk about friends—how to get them, how to keep them, how to get rid of them, and how to be one. This TalkSheet will help your group discuss friendship from a Christian perspective.

OPENER

If your group is large enough, play the famous friends game. Give everyone a slip of paper with one half of a well-known duo written on it. Examples include the President and First Lady, Mickey and Minnie Mouse, Donald and Daffy Duck, Kermit the Frog and Miss Piggy, and so on. They have to find their partners without saying anything or showing anyone their slips of paper. They'll have to act out their characters in order to find their match.

Or you can play that same game, but with pictures from magazines, newspapers or the Internet. Paste the picture on a piece of paper, then cut the picture in half, so that each kid gets one half of the picture. They must find the person who has the other half of their picture without talking.

THE DISCUSSION, BY THE NUMBERS

1. Have the kids talk about their friends and why they are good friends. If they don't want to talk about specific people, have them tell what qualities close friends have.

2. Discuss each item on the list and ask for volunteers to share their answers. Some won't feel comfortable sharing, so you may want to create new questions about each, like—How can a person make new friends? Why do you think parents might not like your friends? Or use a general question like, "What did you learn from these statements?" Some might way that they realize they would like to have more friends. Talk about why it's hard to make new friends—especially outside their clique or current group of friends.

3. Use this attention-getter to discuss trust among friendships. Your kids may not understand why friends would betray or hurt them. Talk about respect in friendships and how fragile friendships can be. How would they react if this happened to them?

4. Ask for some to share their completed sentences and then talk about why God created friendships. Remind them that their relationship with God is a friendship, too. How can God help your kids strengthen their current friendships and make new ones?

THE CLOSE

Read Proverbs 18:24—"A good friend shows himself friendly." In other words, if your kids want to have good friends, then they need to be a good friend. What does it take to be a good friend? Friendships, like all relationships are two sided—they need mutual respect, consideration, and effort.

Point out that the Bible is filled with stories of friendship—in fact, Jesus himself had many good friends, a close group of men and women with whom he spent a lot of time. He was the perfect example of true friendship—loving, patient, giving. He showed all of us how to relate to others in positive ways.

Jesus also wants to be our friend—he sticks with us through it all. Remind your kids that if they have Christ as their friend, they'll be part of a family—a circle of Christian friends. That's what the church (and this youth group) is all about! They are the friends of Jesus and need each other for support and encouragement.

Close with a prayer, asking God to bless our friendships. Give your kids time to pray for their specific relationships and for their friends.

MORE

● Friendships take work! They need to be nurtured in order to grow. Challenge your kids to nurture their friendships this week. Have them send each of their close friends a postcard or e-mail telling them how much their friendship means to them. Have them go out of their way to encourage their friends and then thank God for the friends he's given them.

● What do your kids need to work on to be better friends to others? Challenge them throughout the week to think of three things that they'd like to work on in their friendships. Do they need more patience? More kindness? Use 1 Corinthians 13:1-13 to guide them. What would your kids like to change about themselves?

LIVIN' IT UP

1. List five things you think are fun to do.

   Now, put an X by those you've done recently.

2. Give your opinion on the following eight items—**Y (yes)** or **N (no)**?
   ___ It is fun being a Christian.
   ___ My life is boring.
   ___ Christians have a different kind of fun than non-Christians.
   ___ I need more excitement in my life because I'm a Christian.
   ___ When I'm having fun, I sometimes don't care what might happen to me.
   ___ I would rather have fun with a few friends than a large crowd.
   ___ Non-Christian kids don't really have fun—they just think that they do.
   ___ Most fun things are either sinful or unhealthy.

3. Fill this out: I could have more fun if **I changed places** with—

   Why?

4. Read the following Bible verses and write what **you think** each says about having fun.

   Deuteronomy 12:7

   Ecclesiastes 11:9

LIVIN' IT UP [h a v i n g   f u n]

THIS WEEK

Some young people don't know how to have fun. They're facing so many adult pressures and issues that many youth forget how to play. Others play too much and too hard. Teenagers have mistaken fun with substance abuse and other unhealthy activities. Kids who see someone acting spontaneous or a little crazy automatically assume that the person is drunk or high. Teenagers today don't recognize true play—they need to learn how to have fun creatively and safely.

OPENER

This is your chance to make this discussion fun! Choose a few fun games and let the group play them. There are several store bought games like Outburst or Scattegories that are great for large groups. You could also check out the Ideas Library books (Youth Specialties). Or have your kids bring in their favorite music or video (but be sure you screen what is shown or played!). You may also want to have your kids or parents bring in a variety of fun food—pizza, soda, chips, cookies, or ice cream sundaes.

Or, you may want to plan a random fun event, such as a short scavenger hunt or another activity that you normally wouldn't do at a typical meeting.

THE DISCUSSION, BY THE NUMBERS

1. Brainstorm with your kids and form a list of the things that they consider to be fun. The list can include activities, events, and other items—both positive and negative. Keep the list visible on a poster board or whiteboard to refer to later. Ask the kids to share which ones they've placed an X beside, showing which ones they've done lately. In what ways were those activities fun? Which activities have they never done? Why not?

2. Take these statements one at a time and ask for a show of hands on each one. Ask the reasons behind each one. Find out why (or why not) Christians have fun. Why do they think their life is boring? Or why do they think God is against fun? Many young people expect to have constant excitement in their lives. Some young people are always living on the edge and are headed for trouble. Partying, drinking, smoking, and drug abuse has become a major sport for many, even among middle schoolers. Wholesome fun is healthy—misguided fun can be dangerous.

3. Ask why they chose the person named in this item. What is it about the person that makes them think they would have more fun if they were that person? Could they ever become like that person?

4. You might wish to divide the kids into smaller groups to decide what each of these passages has to say about fun. What does God say about fun? Do they think heaven will be fun?

THE CLOSE

Point out that God does want us to have fun! He isn't a cosmic killjoy—or a corrective parent—sitting up in heaven with a frown on his face. He wants us to enjoy life at its fullest. That's why he created all the things in life that are enjoyable. He's the creator of life and he knows what's best for us and how we can get the most out of life. Read Philippians 4:4 where Paul encourages us to rejoice.

It's possible to party without getting into trouble. Your kids will probably encounter many situations as they grow older when they'll face decisions about drugs and alcohol. Emphasize that having fun is not synonymous with getting wasted. Losing control, getting sick, and risking irreversible brain damage is not fun. Encourage your kids to pursue activities without doing anything they'll regret later.

MORE

● Have your kids share stories or bring in pictures of some times when they've had the most fun. Who were they with? What did they do that made the time so much fun?

● Plan a big fun event with your kids during a weekend or school break. This could include a special event, a trip to an amusement park, or an overnight camping trip. Let your budget and your creativity guide you. You may want to have a special fundraiser with your group to raise money for this. Then go and have a rockin' time with your kids!

● Have your kids do some research of fun things to do in the area. This is more difficult if you live in a small town! Have them check out the Internet for information on events or things going on in your area. Or on a whiteboard or poster board, brainstorm together fun activities that they could do. Challenge them to think creatively (not just renting movies), but do think of ways that they can spice up their fun times, even if it is low key.

THE BIG BOOK

1. **Check** the following statements that are true for you.
   - ❏ The Bible is my favorite book! I read it every day.
   - ❏ I try to read the Bible once a day.
   - ❏ I read the Bible only when I go to church.
   - ❏ The Bible is boring and I never read it.
   - ❏ I have my own Bible.
   - ❏ I have trouble understanding the Bible.
   - ❏ I want to read the Bible but I never have.

2. What is your **favorite** Bible story? Why?

3. **Draw a line** through the statements below that you think aren't in the Bible.
   - a. God helps those who help themselves.
   - b. The Lord works in mysterious ways, his wonders to perform.
   - c. I can do everything through [Christ] who gives me strength.
   - d. In all things God works for the good of those who love him.
   - e. Cleanliness is next to godliness.
   - f. Do unto others before they do unto you.
   - g. Do not judge, or you too will be judged.
   - h. All men are created equal.
   - i. Shop till you drop.

4. Read these statements and decide whether you **agree** or **disagree**.
   - _____a. The Bible is a book of rules.
   - _____b. Science has proved there are mistakes in the Bible.
   - _____c. The Old Testament doesn't apply to the modern world of today.
   - _____d. The Bible is God's Word.
   - _____e. The main theme of the Bible is the story of Jesus Christ.

5. Summarize each of these verses in **five words or less**.
   - Psalm 119:9-16

   - James 1:21-24

   - 1 Peter 2:1-3

THE BIG BOOK [the Bible]

THIS WEEK

The Bible hasn't changed over thousands of years. But our youth, our culture, and our world have changed drastically. Sometimes it's hard to apply the Bible to our lives. Some youth don't believe the Bible is God's Word or has authority over their lives. This session provides the opportunity to discuss the Bible, what today's young people think of it, and how Christians should use the Bible.

OPENER

Give the kids a quiz. Write the names given below on poster board or whiteboard so that they're visible to all. They must decide which books are in the Bible and which aren't, without looking at the Bible's table of contents.

Hezekiah	Timothy	Judas
Philippians	Matthew	Deuteronomy
Romans	Uzziah	Obadiah
Acts	Nahum	Silas
Laminations	Numbers	Bartholomew

Another good lead-in is to conduct a short Bible quiz, asking questions about Bible characters to test how much your kids know.

THE DISCUSSION, BY THE NUMBERS

1. Let the kids share their feelings about the Bible. Give them the opportunity to be open and honest.

2. Have the kids share their favorite stories. Why are these their favorites?

3. Statements a, b, e, f, h, and i, are not in the Bible. Statement c is Philippians 4:13; d is Romans 8:28; and g is Matthew 7:1

4. Call for a vote on the statements. If there is disagreement, discuss the issue with the group. Ask the kids to explain why they agree or disagree. You'll need to be prepared to give your own views—or the views of your church—in response to some of the questions raised. Allow enough time for questions they might have.

5. Encourage the kids to develop a consistent habit of studying the Bible. Point out that the Bible is God's way of giving them tips for living their lives—it's his way of speaking to them!

THE CLOSE

The Bible is the most sold book in the United States. It's the most sought-after book in countries where Bibles aren't available. In fact, it's banned from some countries. The Bible is God's letter to us. He's got loads of important information for us to read and study.

Brainstorm ways that your kids can get into the Bible. Recommend student versions of Bibles including the *Teen Devotional Bible* (Youth Specialties) or the *New Student Bible* (Zondervan). Encourage them to find a version of the Bible that works for them. If an typical NIV is too hard for them to understand, have them find a version that is easier to read.

Challenge them also to read short bits of the Bible at a time—maybe a few verses or a chapter a day. Have them journal what the verse says to them and how it applies to their lives. See if they can understand how the passage applies to their lives. Sometimes this is hard, sometimes it's easy, but encourage them to stick with it!

You might close by having the kids share their favorite Bible verses with each other. Be sure to share yours and have your other adult leaders do the same. Share why this verse is so special to you and how it applies to your life.

MORE

● There are quite a few stimulating, challenging Bible trivia games available. These are great ways to teach your kids while learning new stuff, too! Play one of these games with your kids or create a Bible trivia game with your group. Have them write their own questions based on the Bible. Or find helpful Bible trivia questions at www.Biblequizzes.com or www.bible-trivia.com.

● Compare different versions of the Bible with your group. This can be interesting and a good way to point out that there's different versions for different people's needs. If you don't have access to different versions, have your kids to some searching on the Internet. There are on-line Bibles available. Assign them verses from different versions and then compare them later on. Discuss why the versions are different. What makes some easier to read than others? Does it still say the same thing?

● You may want to set up an e-mail distribution list with your group and e-mail them a verse every few days. Include a few simple questions for them to think about when they read the verses. Most kids will read their Bibles, but they need encouragement to do it! Also, you may want to start a small group Bible study and discussion with those who are interested. Check out Youth Specialties resources (www.YouthSpecialties.com) for some kickin' materials, including the Wild Truth series.

THE CHOICE IS YOURS

1. List three big decisions (I mean BIG!) you must make for your future.

2. Place an X next to the two most difficult decisions to make.

   Doing homework or going to youth group
   What video or movie to watch
   What to do after school
   What kind of music to listen to
   What to eat for dinner
   What clothes to wear to school

   When to pray
   What to do on Friday and Saturday nights
   Who to go out with
   What to spend money on
   How much time to spend on the Internet
   Whether or not to have sex

   Now put a ☆ next to the two easiest decisions.

3. Jesse loves to skateboard, but his parents don't like it because the other guys who skate seem like they're up to no good. He disagrees with his parents and decides to skateboard with his friends anyway. What do you think of Jesse's decision?

4. Which of the following would help you make wise decisions?
   ❏ Asking your parents for advice
   ❏ Praying about it
   ❏ Waiting a few days before deciding
   ❏ Reading your horoscope
   ❏ Asking a friend
   ❏ Thinking about the consequences
   ❏ Deciding as quickly as possible

   ❏ Flipping a coin
   ❏ Going along with the crowd's decision
   ❏ Letting someone else decide for you
   ❏ Finding Bible verses that give direction
   ❏ Going with what feels right
   ❏ Asking in an online chatroom
   ❏ Other—

5. What do these verses have to say about **making decisions**?

   Matthew 6:22-23

   John 14:15-17

   Romans 13:11-14

   Galatians 6:7-8

THE CHOICE IS YOURS [decision-making]

THIS WEEK

Junior high and middle school kids develop a strong desire to make their own decisions. They start to feel more independent and are given more freedoms as they get older. But, they also face lots of decisions—with little decision-making experience. This TalkSheet explores decision-making from a Christian perspective.

OPENER

Start by gift wrapping some items in different paper. Include a variety of different items, such as something valuable (gift certificate or five dollar bill), not valuable (a rock or a plastic cup), ugly or strange (like a white elephant gift), and so on. Announce that one package contains something that they'd like, another contains something worthless, and at least one other has nothing at all. Divide them into the same number of groups as the number of packages. Then they must decide which they would like to have. They cannot touch the gifts before deciding. Once they've made up their minds, decide (by drawing straws, picking numbers, or flipping a coin) which group gets to choose first, second, third, and so on.

Before they open the gifts, ask them how easy or difficult it was to decide? Why or why not? Then let them open the packages and see if they made good choices.

THE DISCUSSION, BY THE NUMBERS

1. Have the kids share the big decisions they anticipate making. Find out which ones the group has in common. When will they need to make these decisions? Which ones are more important than the others?

2. Ask the kids to share the toughest decisions and the easiest. Why are some more hard to make than others? Ask them to come up with any that weren't listed.

3. What advice do they have for Jesse? Use this attention-getter to discuss the importance of listening to adult advice. Help kids try to understand the parents' point of view. Why would the parents be concerned? Does Jesse have the ability to decide for himself what he can or can't do? If not, when does he have that right? Have the group brainstorm ways to get parents to listen to them and to arrive at a compromise.

4. Use this item to talk about the practical how-tos of making decisions: (1) gather all the facts, (2) consider the alternatives, (3) get some good advice, (4) pray, (5) think of every consequence possible, and (6) choose the best possible option.

5. How do these verses apply to practical situations in the lives of today's teens? Encourage them to think about God's perspective when making decisions. How will their decisions impact others?

THE CLOSE

Big decisions are really a combination of little decisions. The choices your kids make today will set the foundation for their future. Encourage your group to start making wise decisions about little things—they'll be more confident when it is time to make important ones.

It's wise to seek good advice and think about the consequences of decisions. How will this decision affect others around them? How will it affect their own lives? Point out that sometimes there's no right or wrong decision. God may not have an answer for them—he'll force them to make the choice. Encourage your kids to bring their decisions before God and to ask for his wisdom.

MORE

● On a poster board or whiteboard, make a list of all the decisions that your kids are making and will need to make. Then go through each one and brainstorm different ways to make this decision. What consequences or results could come with each decision? Use this activity to point out how important good decision-making is.

● Sometimes kids don't want to hear what adults have to say. They don't realize that parents and other adults have faced the same decisions that they do. You may want to include some other adults in this discussion, including some older high school, college, or post-college adults. Present decisions (from the list above) to each one and have them share how they would decide. Give your kids the chance to ask questions about why they made the decision. Use this time to build respect for others ideas and opinions.

● How do others—people who aren't Christians in junior high or middle school—make decisions? Some go to horoscopes, some to Internet chat rooms, some flip a coin. What other ways are there to make decisions? How would God want us to make our decisions? How can your kids rely on God for decisions—even when they can't hear his voice?

LOOKING UP

1. Place an X on the line to show where your worship service fits the line below.

◆ ▮▮▮▮▮▮▮▮▮▮▮▮▮▮▮▮▮▮▮▮▮▮▮▮▮ ◆

Never boring　　　　**Sometimes boring**　　　　**Always boring**

2. Finish these statements in your own words.

My church's worship service would be **better if**—

One thing I'd like to **change about church** is—

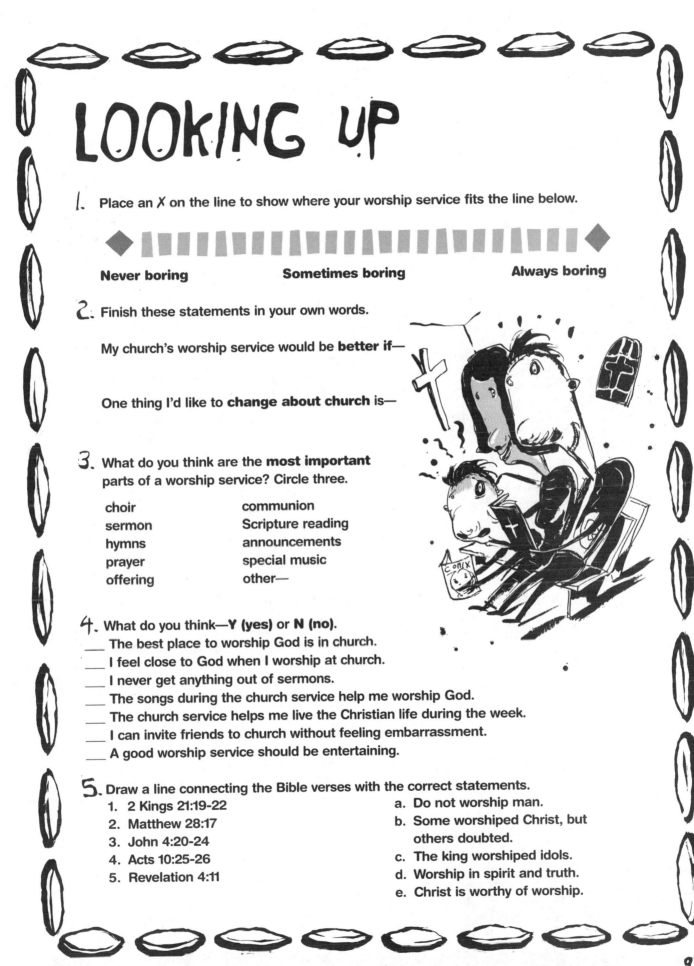

3. What do you think are the **most important** parts of a worship service? Circle three.

choir　　　　　　communion
sermon　　　　　Scripture reading
hymns　　　　　announcements
prayer　　　　　special music
offering　　　　other—

4. What do you think—**Y (yes)** or **N (no)**.
___ The best place to worship God is in church.
___ I feel close to God when I worship at church.
___ I never get anything out of sermons.
___ The songs during the church service help me worship God.
___ The church service helps me live the Christian life during the week.
___ I can invite friends to church without feeling embarrassment.
___ A good worship service should be entertaining.

5. Draw a line connecting the Bible verses with the correct statements.
   1. 2 Kings 21:19-22
   2. Matthew 28:17
   3. John 4:20-24
   4. Acts 10:25-26
   5. Revelation 4:11

   a. Do not worship man.
   b. Some worshiped Christ, but others doubted.
   c. The king worshiped idols.
   d. Worship in spirit and truth.
   e. Christ is worthy of worship.

LOOKING UP [w o r s h i p]

THIS WEEK

Some junior high and middle school kids don't understand the importance and meaning of worship. Maybe they think it's just a boring meeting that their parents force them to attend. Maybe they think it doesn't apply to them all. This TalkSheet provides the opportunity to discuss your church worship service and to encourage your youth group to take their worship service more seriously.

OPENER

Worship isn't just singing, or reading the Bible, or praying. It's a combination of a few different aspects, including listening to God's word and what we can learn about it. We can worship anytime, anywhere—not just in church. Have each of your kids write down on a 3x5 card what worship means to them. Tell them not to include their names, because you're going to collect and read them. Discuss their ideas and why worship is beneficial for Christians. How does worship affect us? How does it affect God?

Brainstorm some ways that kids can worship everyday—not just in church on Sundays. Make a list on a whiteboard or poster board of ways that they can learn more about God during the daily routine. This may include ideas like—saying a prayer in the shower, reading one verse in the morning, listening to some Christian music and thinking about the words, or spending a few minutes of quiet before bed. Communicate that worship isn't just church—it's what goes on in church.

THE DISCUSSION, BY THE NUMBERS

1. Draw a line on a whiteboard or poster board and have each student place an X on the line. Or have one side of the room be "Always boring" and the other "Never boring". Have the kids stand where they placed their X. Then talk about what makes it boring or not boring for them.

2. Ask the kids to share their sentences. (You might wish to show these sentences to your church's worship planning committee. If the kids know this in advance, they might come up with more thoughtful responses.) Let them talk about the parts of the service they don't like. What would they change if they could? What gets them excited to praise God? Remind them that if a part of the service is boring, that's okay—worship is different for everyone, especially in a church with mixed ages.

3. What part of the worship service they enjoy the most and which part they think the church could do without. What do they want more of? What changes would they like to make?

4. These statements focus on different aspects of worship and the worship service. Let the group talk about these and discuss different opinion. Try to save your own comments for the conclusion.

5. How did these verses match up? Ask them to share any new insights they might have gained from reading the passages on worship. What does God think of worship? What is our purpose in worshipping?

THE CLOSE

What are your views of worship? Why is worship important? Consider these ideas—

- Worship is a verb, not a noun. It isn't something we attend in order to be entertained. Instead, it is something we do.
- The worship service brings everyone in the church together, both young and old, which is important. The church is people, the community of God, and it is important for the church to have that common experience together. Corporate worship (worship with others) is one way we acknowledge the church is the body of Christ and how much we need each other.
- Worship is for God, not for us. The question to ask after a worship service is not "Did I like it?" but "Did God like it?" and "Did I do my best for him?" Close by sharing praise and prayer requests to God.

MORE

- Get involved! Plan a worship service with your youth group, and encourage your kids to get involved in different parts of the morning service, such as Bible reading, ushering, offering, greeting, and so on. They are an invaluable part of the church! You may want or need to work with your planning committee to get your youth involved in the services.
- There are several praise and worship rallies and retreats for youth of all ages. One is DCLA—Youth For Christ (www.yfc.org). These mass events give kids a chance to learn and worship with others their age. They often include big-name Christian artists and speakers that give a new light to worship and praising the King. You can find more information on these events and links at www.YouthSpecialties.com.

THE SUNDAY SITUATION

1. **List three things** you could do on Sunday instead of going to church.

2. What do you think is the main reason a person should go to church?

3. What do you think? Read the statements and answer **agree** or **disagree**—
   a. A person should attend church every week._____
   b. You can be a Christian without attending church._____
   c. The church's main concern seems to be taking in money._____
   d. The church is old-fashioned and out of date._____
   e. It doesn't matter which church you attend._____
   f. Our church services are boring._____
   g. I am an important part of our church. _____

4. **Circle** the best answer.
   According to **Hebrews 10:24-25**, attending church is—
   a. optional
   b. unnecessary
   c. the way to get to heaven
   d. habit-forming and encouraging

   Paul, in **1 Corinthians 12:12-14**, compares the church to—
   a. a body
   b. a loaf of bread
   c. a fish
   d. heaven

   Ephesians 4:16 says church members should—
   a. mind their own business
   b. grow in love
   c. take communion once a week
   d. be critical of each other

THE SUNDAY SITUATION [church]

THIS WEEK

If you've discussed worship, then you've talked about church, too. Sometimes kids get church and worship mixed up, or they clump the two together. Although they are intertwined, this TalkSheet is designed to define what the church is, create discussion about the church, and encourage young people to be involved in their church.

OPENER

Start by asking your kids what's important about Sunday. You might like to keep a list for them to see. Ask them why God made Sundays. Why do they, as people, need Sundays? How do their families observe Sunday? Is Sunday any different than any other day? You'll most likely get many different responses to this. Point out that Sunday is a gift from God—a full day to rest and relax from our normal routine. Although some people have to work, depending on their jobs, why is it important to make Sundays different?

Now ask them what church is. Make this a different column to separate the two. Is church only for coming together for Sunday school, a sermon, some songs, or some post-service snacks? What is church for? Why does God want us to be part of a church family? Point out that the church encourages our spiritual growth by letting us meet with other people. It holds us accountable for our lives and for making Sunday different.

THE DISCUSSION, BY THE NUMBERS

1. Encourage the kids to share the activities they chose. Talk about the importance (or unimportance) of each in relation to church attendance. Many of your junior high and middle school kids attend church because they are forced to. Ask them, "If you were not forced to go to church, do you think you would still go?" Why or why not? In what ways is church a good experience or bad one for them?

2. What are the reasons people should go to church? You may want to list them on the whiteboard or poster board. Have them choose the one they think is the most important. Point out there are several reasons to attend church—church shouldn't be an obligation! It should be something that they do for God to know him better.

3. Ask the kids to vote on each of these statements according to their answers on the TalkSheet. Let them discuss the things they agree or don't agree on. Let them defend their points of view. Allow them the freedom to express their opinions without others being judgmental. Then, share your point of view in the conclusion. You might wish to focus on the last statement, because many junior high and middle school kids don't feel needed in the church. Suggest ways for them to become more involved.

4. Did the group match up the correct verses and statements? You may want to check it out with the group and re-read each verse. How does God feel about Sunday? Why does he want us to go to church?

THE CLOSE

As you close this session, you might wish to emphasize the following, as well as any other points you'd like to add—

- The church isn't a building or a service to attend. People could meet in a shack and still be in a church! The church is the people of God coming together. When a young person becomes a Christian, the person becomes part of the church, the body of Christ.
- The purpose of the church isn't to entertain us or to provide fun activities. We come to church to learn about God, to grow in faith, and to worship him. This requires some effort and the desire to do these things.
- Young people aren't just the church of tomorrow—they are an important part of the church today! Encourage them to get involved in the life of the church. Brainstorm ways they can become more involved and have your worship leaders help them get involved.

MORE

● How well do your kids know the church? You may want to give your group a church quiz. A few of these might require them to find answers from other church members. Sample questions may include things like—
⇨ Name a missionary sponsored by our church, and the country where he or she serves.
⇨ What is our pastor's middle name?
⇨ What is the name of the church's newsletter?
⇨ What year was our church founded?
● Challenge your kids to give your church leaders feedback on the church services. What do your kids like or not like about the worship? How can the church get your kids involved more or meet the needs of your youth. Encourage them to voice their opinions through letter or e-mails and take an active roll in what goes on.

TO DO OR NOT TO DO

1. **Right** or **wrong**? Rate each on a scale of **1-15** (1 being really bad, 15 being okay).

   ___ Stealing
   ___ Wasting your money
   ___ Skipping youth group
   ___ Hitting a sibling
   ___ Getting an abortion
   ___ Doing drugs
   ___ Hanging out with the wrong crowd
   ___ Ignoring the advice of adults or parents

   ___ Surfing the Internet
   ___ Not doing your personal devotions
   ___ Being tardy for a class
   ___ Cussing when you're angry
   ___ Cheating on the test you forgot about
   ___ Drinking when you're underage
   ___ Going too far with physical intimacy

2. When you believe something is wrong and you do it anyway—

   How do you feel?

   Why do you think you do it anyway?

3. Complete the following sentence with the ending most appropriate for you.
   I'm able to live the way I should—
   a. all of the time.
   b. most of the time.
   c. some of the time.
   d. none of the time.

4. Ryan knew he shouldn't have cheated on the exam. But it was the *only* way he was going to pass this class. Besides, no one saw him looking at notes in his lap and sneaking answers off Todd's paper. Ryan concludes that what he did wasn't so bad. After all, nobody is perfect all the time.

   What do you think of Ryan's behavior?

   Why did Ryan make excuses for what he did?

   What would you do if you were in Ryan's situation?

5. Rewrite **Romans 7:15** in your own words.

TO DO OR NOT TO DO [values and behavior]

THIS WEEK

Values. Parents try to instill them. Teachers try to promote them. The church tries to uphold them. Values define what one believes and what one does. This TalkSheet is designed to help you discuss the struggles junior high and middle school kids face and how they shape their values. Use this discussion with a group that interacts well, respects each other, and has a deep level of sharing and concern.

OPENER

How hard is it stick with your beliefs? Well, try the human knot activity. Ask the males in your group sit or stand together in a huge human knot with their arms and legs locked. Now the challenging part—let the girls try to pull them apart. A few rules, though—no hitting, pinching, or kicking—only pulling. Give them a few minutes. Then debrief with your group to talk about struggles. What was hard about trying to pull them apart? Was it hard for the guys to stick together when they were being pulled away? What made the guys stick together so tightly? Did the girls want to give up?

THE DISCUSSION, BY THE NUMBERS

1. Have the kids share their beliefs on these items and think of others to all. Communicate that people can believe something but not live it. Which of these are hard to do? What temptations or pressures come with each one? Be careful not to lay a guilt trip on your kids.

2. Most of the young people will probably say they feel guilty. Explain that guilt is God's way of pointing out behaviors that don't match our values. Don't let them get away with "I don't know"—ask them why they give in to pressures. Why is it hard to stick with our values? What can we do to stick with our values?

3. Without having them raise their hands, ask if anyone checked all of the time. If they did—they're wrong! Point out that no one is perfect. If anyone checked none of the time—oh, they're in trouble! What is keeping them from living their values? How hard is it to live according to our values? Challenge them to live their beliefs most of the time. This takes commitment and work. It also takes patience and help from God.

4. Discuss this attention-getter, and ask the kids to rank Ryan's actions on a scale of 1 to 10 with 10 as the best. Most of them will choose a number somewhere in between. Point out that most of our decisions fall in a gray area. Rationalizing our behavior isn't the way. God doesn't settle for excuses—but he does give forgiveness. Ask your kids if they've had or heard of similar situations. What did they or the person do?

5. Ask the kids to read their paraphrases. Point out Paul felt the same way they do! They are responsible to God and ourselves for our decisions.

THE CLOSE

How well do your kids walk their talk? Encourage your kids to think through their values. What can they do today, and from now on, to live what they believe? What changes do they need to make? Brainstorm how they can put their beliefs into practice. Remind them that the more they do it, the easier it is.

Stress the fact that failure is normal. Being a Christian doesn't mean that they are expected to be perfect. It means when they do fail, they don't give up. It means they keep trying to improve ourselves and how they live. God is there for us, waiting for us to come back to him.

Finally, close with a prayer. Challenge your kids to ask God to help them with struggles or areas where they need strength to live their values. If they need to ask for forgiveness, encourage them to pray silently. Communicate that God takes guilt away and that he loves us no matter what.

MORE

● The Bible is full of characters who struggled with their values. A few examples include Moses (who killed an Egyptian), David (who committed adultery and murder), and Jonah (who ran away from God). Have your group find some of these example and talk about them together. What were their struggles and what happened to them? Share these findings and talk about how God used these people, in spite of their struggles and failings.

● You may want to take some time to talk about values in the media. Make a list of values that your kids see on TV, in the movies, on the Internet, on the radio, and so on. How do these values compare to the values Christians are to live by? In what ways do your kids face these values at school or at home? What can they do to resist these pressures? Have them bring in specific examples of a value that the media promotes. How much do your kids believe what they see and hear? Challenge them to keep their eyes open to contradicting values.

GOT SPIRIT?

1. **Circle** the words listed below you think best describe the Holy Spirit—

friend   miracle performer   teacher
healer   tempter   counselor
creator   helper   universal power
stranger   ghost   electric

2. How would you respond to this statement—**true** or **false**?
In the Christian faith, the Holy Spirit is not as important as Jesus or God.

3. **Check** the things you think the Holy Spirit does for you.
   - ❏ Gives you power to live a successful Christian life
   - ❏ Makes you popular
   - ❏ Teaches you and helps you mature as a Christian
   - ❏ Gives you spiritual gifts
   - ❏ Makes you better than others
   - ❏ Helps you perform miracles
   - ❏ Gives you peace and comfort
   - ❏ Helps you make the right decisions
   - ❏ Takes away your problems
   - ❏ Keeps bad things from happening to you
   - ❏ Nothing
   - ❏ Helps you resist temptation
   - ❏ Gives you love for people you don't like
   - ❏ Gives you hope
   - ❏ Makes you feel good inside
   - ❏ Gives you money
   - ❏ Helps you get good grades
   - ❏ Is your conscience

4. Read **Galatians 5:22-26** and list the fruits of the Spirit below.

Put a by the one you think you need the **most**.

GOT SPIRIT? [the Holy Spirit]

THIS WEEK

For most junior high and middle school kids, the Holy Spirit is a mystery. They can relate to God the Father and God the Son, but they aren't clear about God the Holy Spirit. It's hard to understand why or how God can be three different people at the same time. This TalkSheet gives you the chance to discuss the role the Holy Spirit plays in the life of a Christian.

OPENER

The Holy Spirit is God living inside each person. The Spirit is a storehouse of power who gives people strength and wisdom to live the Christian life. To illustrate, empty a small can of shaving cream in a bowl. It's amazing how much stuff comes out of one can! But, to get the stuff to come out, you had to push the button. The same thing happens with the Holy Spirit in us. The more they push that button—pray, sing, get into the Bible, and spend time with God—the more they overflow with the Spirit. If they have God in their hearts, they have the Holy Spirit.

THE DISCUSSION, BY THE NUMBERS

1. Ask the kids to share their choices and explain why they chose them. Try to keep this positive and don't focus on the wrong answers. This is a learning experience for your kids. Ask for other suggestions that they might use to describe the Holy Spirit.

2. You'll probably get mostly true responses, but some wrong answers too. Again, be careful not to be hard on those who answered false. This is a good place to explain the doctrine of the Trinity. All three persons of the Trinity are equal because they are the same. They are all God, just in different parts. You may want to consult your church's statement of faith, or look up the following Bible verses—John 14:15-31; Romans 8:1-7; and 1 Corinthians 2:6-16.

3. As the group shares their answers, focus on those things specifically mentioned in the Bible. Here is a partial list—comforts us, John 14:16-17; convicts us of sin, John 16:8-11; teaches and guides us, John 16:13-15; prays for us, Romans 8:26; gives us spiritual gifts, 1 Corinthians 12:7; leads us, Galatians 5:18.

4. Ask volunteers to state why they chose one fruit of the Spirit over all the others. What fruit do they need to have more of? How can they work on this?

THE CLOSE

The Holy Spirit plays a vital role in the life of Christians. He encourages us, strengthens us, and fills us with all the fruits—love, patience, kindness, self-control, and so on.

One way to illustrate this with an object lesson is to use a glove. It can't do anything without your hand in it. But when you put your hand in the glove, it can do anything your brain wants your hand to do. It can pick up things, wave, scratch your head, and much more. In the same way, when the Holy Spirit is in us and works in our lives, we can do anything God wants us to do. Challenge your kids to ask God to take more control of their lives and to fill them with his Spirit. The closer they are to God, the more his Spirit works in us.

MORE

- What are the top three questions that your group has about the Holy Spirit? You may want to talk about these with your senior pastor or another adult. Or have groups of your kids find one piece of information on the Holy Spirit. Encourage them to ask a parent, teacher, pastor, sibling, look through their Bible, or look on the Internet. How would they describe the Holy Spirit?
- Break your group into smaller groups. Have them brainstorm or think of an analogy to help them understand the Trinity. Some examples are an egg (white, yolk, shell), an apple (skin, inside, core) a candle (wax, wick, flame) or water (ice, liquid, steam). There are others, too, and you might be surprised what your kids come up with. Have them explain why the idea makes sense to them and how it helps them understand the Trinity better.
- Or dig into the Bible to find some info! Break your group up into three groups and have each group find verses that describe each part of the Trinity—God, Jesus, and the Spirit. Compare these verses and descriptions of each part. How does the Bible describe each one? Is each part the same? What are the differences between them? Is one more powerful than another?

STRESSED OUT

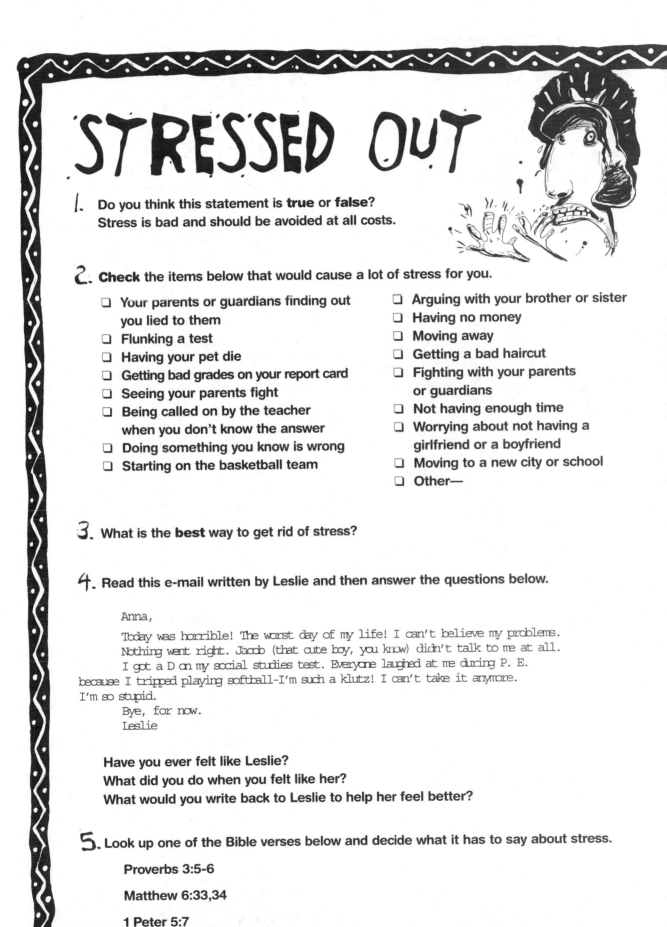

1. Do you think this statement is **true** or **false**?
   Stress is bad and should be avoided at all costs.

2. **Check** the items below that would cause a lot of stress for you.

   - ❏ Your parents or guardians finding out you lied to them
   - ❏ Flunking a test
   - ❏ Having your pet die
   - ❏ Getting bad grades on your report card
   - ❏ Seeing your parents fight
   - ❏ Being called on by the teacher when you don't know the answer
   - ❏ Doing something you know is wrong
   - ❏ Starting on the basketball team

   - ❏ Arguing with your brother or sister
   - ❏ Having no money
   - ❏ Moving away
   - ❏ Getting a bad haircut
   - ❏ Fighting with your parents or guardians
   - ❏ Not having enough time
   - ❏ Worrying about not having a girlfriend or a boyfriend
   - ❏ Moving to a new city or school
   - ❏ Other—

3. What is the **best** way to get rid of stress?

4. Read this e-mail written by Leslie and then answer the questions below.

   > Anna,
   > Today was horrible! The worst day of my life! I can't believe my problems.
   > Nothing went right. Jacob (that cute boy, you know) didn't talk to me at all.
   > I got a D on my social studies test. Everyone laughed at me during P. E.
   > because I tripped playing softball-I'm such a klutz! I can't take it anymore.
   > I'm so stupid.
   > Bye, for now.
   > Leslie

   Have you ever felt like Leslie?
   What did you do when you felt like her?
   What would you write back to Leslie to help her feel better?

5. Look up one of the Bible verses below and decide what it has to say about stress.

   Proverbs 3:5-6

   Matthew 6:33,34

   1 Peter 5:7

STRESSED OUT [stress]

THIS WEEK

Stress is a fact of life for young people and adults. Unfortunately teenagers today have more stress than ever before. Many of these stressors are put on them by parents, peers, teachers, and the church. Media tells teenagers one thing, while their parents and church tell them another. They must balance friends, schoolwork, athletics, family and fun all at the same time. This TalkSheet will help your group talk about stress and how they can handle it as Christians.

OPENER

Perform a stress test on a balloon. Have one of your kids blow the balloon up until it's ready to pop (have them make it pop if you want!). Stop just before it's popped and have the volunteer let some air out. Ask them if they've ever felt like that balloon. How many of them feel so stressed out that they feel they're going to explode? Have they seen their friends or parents reach this point?

You can also play a game of Jenga, the game of wooden pieces that are stacked on top of each other. Players pull pieces out of the stack and restack them. Finally, the whole thing topples over. This is true of stress—we have so much stacked up in our lives and so much demanded from us. Sometimes we can't take it, and we feel like crashing.

THE DISCUSSION, BY THE NUMBERS

1. Ask for a show of hands on this true or false question. Explain the best answer would be false because (1) some stress is normal and actually beneficial—the anxiety caused by stress is a warning system that signals us respond to whatever is causing the stress; and (2) avoidance of all stress is extremely unhealthy. For example, some people turn to drugs or alcohol as a way of escaping stress, which creates even more stress to themselves and others.

2. This activity brings the topic closer to home. Rather than having the kids tell you which items they checked, ask how many checked more than three. More than five? More than eight? You might ask the group to vote on the one or two items they think most teens are faced with. Why is this so stressful? What pressures are the hardest to deal with?

3. Have the group share their ideas on this. Talk about practical things they can do when they feel overwhelmed by the pressures in their lives.

4. A good way to deal with this attention-getter is to have two kids role-play Leslie and a friend who is trying to help her. Or, you can play Leslie and the entire group can advise you. You can give excuses like, "I already tried that" and "That would never work for me," to keep the ideas coming.

5. Divide the kids into smaller groups for this exercise. Each group should take a different Bible verse and come up with a statement about what the Bible says concerning coping with stress.

THE CLOSE

Emphasize the fact that stress is normal, but too much unresolved stress can wear them down, both physically and mentally. Stress makes people sick and caused frustration and depression.

Make sure your kids understand that it's important to deal with stress, worry, or pressure. If they feel overwhelmed, to the point where they are feeling depressed or sick, they have to let it out. Challenge them to find a trusted adult who they can talk to and let the pressure out. Encourage them to come to you with questions about stress in their lives.

Encourage them to find other ways to deal with stress—to exercise, write down their feelings, play music, or read a book. Stress can be good, but don't let it make you lazy! Too much stress isn't always an excuse to get out of doing what you're supposed to do. Encourage them to ask God for patience and peace when they are feeling stressed out. Prayer is the best way to vent to God and lay situations before him.

MORE

● Some of your kids may have family members or friends who are abused by their parents or siblings. Stress, like anger, is never an excuse for anyone to hit or abuse anyone. Communicate that if your kids ever face an abusive situation, or know a friend who does, they must find a trusted adult immediately. Physical, sexual, and substance abuse is against the law—it's a serious crime. Encourage them to find an adult to talk to and remind them that you are there for them anytime.

● Plan a fun, de-stressing activity for and with your kids. Do something fun and spontaneous with the group. Surprise them with a dessert night, a movie night, or a trip to the beach. Make sure that everyone is welcome and included.

● When someone is stressed out, they need to be encouraged. Challenge your kids to encourage three people during the week—friends, family members, or teachers. Have them send an e-mail or letter encouraging the person and telling them what they appreciate about them.

USER

1. What do you think of when you hear the words **doing drugs**?

2. What do you think? **true or false**—Parents should talk about drugs with their kids.

3. Tyrone and Craig see some of their friends smoking marijuana behind school. Tyrone and Craig are invited to join. Tyrone jumps right in and looks at Craig.

If you were Craig, **what** would you do?

What are the **risks** of giving in to Tyrone?

4. Give your opinion to the statements below—**Yes**, **No,** or **Maybe**.
a. Most drugs are harmless._____
b. If a friend offered me drugs, I could say no without any problem._____
c. If a person's friends are users, then that person needs new friends._____
d. Teenagers who use dope are more likely to get into trouble than those who don't._____
e. It's okay to use drugs as long as you don't become addicted._____

5. What do you think each verse has to say about **using drugs**?

Romans 12:1-2

1 Corinthians 3:16-17

1 Corinthians 10:31

USER [d r u g s]

THIS WEEK

America is a drugged society. Drugs are everywhere—from the medicine cabinet to the streets of our cities. Young people—including junior high and middle school kids—face tremendous pressure to experiment with drugs. This TalkSheet encourages an open discussion about drugs, dealing with the risks and consequences for people, including Christians.

You don't want this session to be like your kids' school health class. Your goal is to talk about drugs in light of Christ. Some of your kids may be using drugs, may have tried drugs, or have friends or family members who do. Be extra sensitive to your group members and be careful not to sound too judgmental.

OPENER

You may want to start by reading an article or statistics from a magazine or from the newspaper about drug abuse. They're on the Internet as well, if you spend a few minutes searching. Read the story out loud or have your kids take turns reading the story. Afterwards, ask them for their reactions to the article.

Or on a whiteboard or poster board, make a list of all the different drugs that your kids know of—they might be able to list quite a few. Have an additional list ready—you can find these on the Internet as well. Check out the National Institute of Drug Abuse (www.nida.nih.gov/NIDAHome1.html), the Addiction Research Foundation (www.arf.org/isd/info.html), or The National Clearinghouse for Alcohol and Drug Information (www.health.org/pubs/qdocs/). Drugs include anything that alters the body and mind, including caffeine and paint thinner—not just the hard-core street drugs.

THE DISCUSSION, BY THE NUMBERS

1. Write the words "drug abuse" on the poster board or whiteboard. Underneath, write down all the things offered in response to this question.

2. Ask how many of your group have discussed drugs with their parents or guardians and what was said. Why might it not be easy for parents to talk about this? Challenge your teens to talk with the adults in their about drugs. Many adults have had exposure to drugs as well, especially when they were young.

3. Use this attention-getter to illustrate how peer pressure creates a false need to try drugs. Have the kids share their responses to this situation and ask if they have ever experienced or know of a similar one. You might have them role-play the action, to give them practice handling a similar occasion.

4. Have the kids reveal their answers to these questions with a show of hands. If everyone agrees, move on to the next one. If there's disagreement or doubt, discuss the issue. Allow them to share their responses.

5. You might divide the kids into smaller groups and assign one Scripture to each. They can then decide as a unit what each passage has to say about drugs, sharing the conclusion with the entire group. Point out the Bible does not specifically mention drugs—there's no verse that says, "Thou shall not do drugs." But the Bible verses do give us clear principles upon which to make decisions about destructive choices such as drugs.

THE CLOSE

Using drugs is not only illegal, but it is deadly. Even those that which are relatively inexpensive and readily available—like glue, paint, and other chemicals that some teenagers use to get high.

Drug pushers like to get teenagers hooked at an early age—often offering them free drugs for a month, with bonuses for other kids they can influence to try them. Once they're hooked, victims have no control. The dealer gets what he wants—money. The victim gets permanent brain damage.

Christians recognize that happiness and peace come only from following Christ. Why do they want to harm our bodies and minds, when God can fill us up?

If your kids are having problems with drugs, or if they know someone who is, or if they have questions, encourage them to talk with a school counselor, parent, teacher, or you. The sooner they quit, the better. Drugs are addictive—the more they do it, the more they'll need to keep doing it.

MORE

● How much do your kids know about drugs? Are they aware of the types, the names, and the effects? You may ask groups to do some research on the kinds of drugs readily available, including the street names of drugs and what effect they have on the body and on behavior.

● In groups, have your kids consider if they were a school counselor or principal, how would they persuade kids to say no to drugs. Have your kids brainstorm in groups about how they'd to do this. Maybe have them create an anti-drug slogan. Challenge them to write a letter to their school counselor or principal, explaining what they've talked about and how they can get involved in an anti-drug campaign in their school.

JESUS GIVEAWAY

1. Do you think that this statement is **true** or **false**? Most of my friends are not interested in hearing about Jesus Christ.

2. If you shared Christ with your friends at school, what do you think they'd do? **Circle one**.
   - Laugh at me
   - Blow me off
   - Be polite but do nothing
   - Show some interest
   - Become Christians
   - Other—

3. Everybody at school knew Rita believed in Jesus and went to church regularly. Some kids made fun of her; others ignored her. If your friends made fun of Rita while you were with them, **what would you do**?

4. Choose **two effective** ways to share Christ with your friends (and others, too).
   - ❏ Quote Bible verses when friends ask you questions
   - ❏ Hand out gospel tracts in the cafeteria
   - ❏ Be an honest and trustworthy person
   - ❏ Carry a Bible around with you
   - ❏ Stick to your morals
   - ❏ Pray for your friends
   - ❏ Whenever a teacher calls on you for an answer, respond with "JESUS!"
   - ❏ Bring your friend with you to youth group
   - ❏ Wear a Christian T-shirt
   - ❏ Stand up on your desk at school and preach the gospel
   - ❏ Listen to Christian music
   - ❏ Paint a big "J.C." on the side of your school

5. Try to **match** up the following sayings of Jesus—
   1. Go and make disciples
   2. You are the light
   3. I will make you fishers
   4. You will be my witnesses

   a. ...of the world (Matthew 5:14-16).
   b. ...of men (Mark 1:17).
   c. ...of all nations (Matthew 28:18-20).
   d. ...to the ends of the earth (Acts 1:8).

JESUS GIVEAWAY [w i t n e s s i n g]

THIS WEEK

Sometimes it's not easy for teenagers to share their faith with others. It's difficult to explain their beliefs when others are questioning them. Both adults and teens struggle with being a witness, without coming off as radicals. This TalkSheet gives you and your group the opportunity to talk about witnessing and to practice sharing the Christian faith.

OPENER

In this activity, create a role-play situation with you and your group. You may want to get some info in advance to use against your group. Find some facts about other religions and their beliefs. Then present a situation like this—you are a foreign exchange student from India. You grew up in the Hindu religion. Now you're living with an American family that goes to church and worships God. You learned at home that Christians believe in heaven, not reincarnation. You're confused and feel a bit threatened by these beliefs. You want to know more, but you aren't sure what to ask.

Break your kids into groups to brainstorm how they would present the gospel to you, the student. What are they going to say? How are they going to defend their beliefs? Have them write down some points. Then bring the groups together and begin the role-play by confronting them about seeing one of them reading the Bible. Have your kids explain their beliefs to you. Question the kids and get them thinking about their faith and how to defend what they believe.

THE DISCUSSION, BY THE NUMBERS

1. Have the kids share and explain their answers. List all the reasons why not and all the reasons why on a chalkboard or newsprint.

2. After sharing the answers, ask if the kids have ever actually tried to share their faith with their friends. If so, what happened? If not, why not?

3. This should make a good role-play subject. Have a few of the kids put themselves into this situation and act out their idea of the scenario.

4. Debate the pros and cons of each of the methods listed. Why are some of these better than others? Which ones would work more effectively? Why or why not?

5. Read the verses to find out if the group matched them up correctly. These verses emphasize that Christ wants us to tell others about him.

THE CLOSE

You don't want to make your kids feel guilty with this session. With their self-esteem on the line, teenagers are reluctant to do or say anything that might embarrass them or cause others to reject them. Be careful not to make witnessing sound like burden for being a Christian. Emphasize that being a Christian is a gift that each one can give to someone else. How would they feel if they knew a friend could spend eternity in heaven with them? Does this friend know? Brainstorm creative ways they can be witnesses for Christ in non-threatening ways. They don't have to be Bible experts in order to share Christ with others. They can witness in a lot of non-verbal ways through our actions and what they say to others.

Sharing Christ is a privilege—and a command. It's a responsibility that God give us. It's a way to show others that they are loved and that they love others.

MORE

- Missionaries are spreading the gospel worldwide and they need prayer support. Encourage your group to support missionaries, who are witnesses to others worldwide. Challenge them to pray for missionaries, to write them letters, e-mail, and give money. Consider doing a group fundraiser for the missionaries in your church and get the congregation involved, too.

- Brainstorm for a youth group slogan with your group. This could be a logo, statement, or slogan that reflects their faith somehow. Vote on a slogan and a verse. Then—if you're kids like the idea—make a kickin' youth group T-shirt. When they wear them, have them keep track of the reactions or questions they get at school. Encourage them to use this as a way to explain their beliefs to others who have questions.

  For information on purchasing special order clothing and more, visit the YS links at www.gospelcom.net/ys/central/apparel.html.

RESOURCES FROM YOUTH SPECIALTIES

YOUTH MINISTRY PROGRAMMING

Camps, Retreats, Missions, & Service Ideas (Ideas Library)
Compassionate Kids: Practical Ways to Involve Your Students in Mission and Service
Creative Bible Lessons from the Old Testament
Creative Bible Lessons in 1 & 2 Corinthians
Creative Bible Lessons in John: Encounters with Jesus
Creative Bible Lessons in Romans: Faith on Fire!
Creative Bible Lessons on the Life of Christ
Creative Bible Lessons in Psalms
Creative Junior High Programs from A to Z, Vol. 1 (A-M)
Creative Junior High Programs from A to Z, Vol. 2 (N-Z)
Creative Meetings, Bible Lessons, & Worship Ideas (Ideas Library)
Crowd Breakers & Mixers (Ideas Library)
Downloading the Bible Leader's Guide
Drama, Skits, & Sketches (Ideas Library)
Drama, Skits, & Sketches 2 (Ideas Library)
Dramatic Pauses
Everyday Object Lessons
Games (Ideas Library)
Games 2 (Ideas Library)
Games 3 (Ideas Library)
Good Sex: A Whole-Person Approach to Teenage Sexuality and God
Great Fundraising Ideas for Youth Groups
More Great Fundraising Ideas for Youth Groups
Great Retreats for Youth Groups
Holiday Ideas (Ideas Library)
Hot Illustrations for Youth Talks
More Hot Illustrations for Youth Talks
Still More Hot Illustrations for Youth Talks
Ideas Library on CD-ROM
Incredible Questionnaires for Youth Ministry
Junior High Game Nights
More Junior High Game Nights
Kickstarters: 101 Ingenious Intros to Just about Any Bible Lesson
Live the Life! Student Evangelism Training Kit
Memory Makers
The Next Level Leader's Guide
Play It! Over 150 Great Games for Youth Groups
Roaring Lambs
Special Events (Ideas Library)
Spontaneous Melodramas
Spontaneous Melodramas 2
Student Leadership Training Manual
Student Underground: An Event Curriculum on the Persecuted Church
Super Sketches for Youth Ministry
Talking the Walk
Teaching the Bible Creatively
Videos That Teach
What Would Jesus Do? Youth Leader's Kit
Wild Truth Bible Lessons
Wild Truth Bible Lessons 2
Wild Truth Bible Lessons—Pictures of God
Wild Truth Bible Lessons—Pictures of God 2
Worship Services for Youth Groups

PROFESSIONAL RESOURCES

Administration, Publicity, & Fundraising (Ideas Library)
Dynamic Communicators Workshop
Equipped to Serve: Volunteer Youth Worker Training Course
Help! I'm a Junior High Youth Worker!
Help! I'm a Small-Group Leader!
Help! I'm a Sunday School Teacher!
Help! I'm a Volunteer Youth Worker!
How to Expand Your Youth Ministry
How to Speak to Youth...and Keep Them Awake at the Same Time
Junior High Ministry (Updated & Expanded)
The Ministry of Nurture: A Youth Worker's Guide to Discipling Teenagers
Postmodern Youth Ministry
Purpose-Driven® Youth Ministry
Purpose-Driven® Youth Ministry Training Kit
So That's Why I Keep Doing This! 52 Devotional Stories for Youth Workers
A Youth Ministry Crash Course
Youth Ministry Management Tools
The Youth Worker's Handbook to Family Ministry

ACADEMIC RESOURCES

Four Views of Youth Ministry & the Church
Starting Right: Thinking Theologically About Youth Ministry

DISCUSSION STARTERS

Discussion & Lesson Starters (Ideas Library)
Discussion & Lesson Starters 2 (Ideas Library)
EdgeTV
Get 'Em Talking
Keep 'Em Talking!
Good Sex: A Whole-Person Approach to Teenage Sexuality & God
High School TalkSheets—Updated!
More High School TalkSheets—Updated!
High School TalkSheets Psalms and Proverbs—Updated!
Junior High and Middle School TalkSheets—Updated!
More Junior High and Middle School TalkSheets—Updated!
Junior High and Middle School TalkSheets Psalms and Proverbs—Updated!
Real Kids: Short Cuts
Real Kids: The Real Deal—on Friendship, Loneliness, Racism, & Suicide
Real Kids: The Real Deal—on Sexual Choices, Family Matters, & Loss
Real Kids: The Real Deal—on Stressing Out, Addictive Behavior, Great Comebacks, & Violence
Real Kids: Word on the Street
Unfinished Sentences: 450 Tantalizing Statement-Starters to Get Teenagers Talking & Thinking
What If...? 450 Thought-Provoking Questions to Get Teenagers Talking, Laughing, and Thinking
Would You Rather...? 465 Provocative Questions to Get Teenagers Talking
Have You Ever...? 450 Intriguing Questions Guaranteed to Get Teenagers Talking

ART SOURCE CLIP ART

Stark Raving Clip Art (print)
Youth Group Activities (print)
Clip Art Library Version 2.0 CD-ROM

DIGITAL RESOURCES

Clip Art Library Version 2.0 CD-RPOM
Ideas Library on CD-ROM
Youth Ministry Management Tools

VIDEOS AND VIDEO CURRICULUMS

Dynamic Communicators Workshop
EdgeTV
Equipped to Serve: Volunteer Youth Worker Training Course
The Heart of Youth Ministry: A Morning with Mike Yaconelli
Live the Life! Student Evangelism Training Kit
Purpose-Driven® Youth Ministry Training Kit
Real Kids: Short Cuts
Real Kids: The Real Deal—on Friendship, Loneliness, Racism, & Suicide
Real Kids: The Real Deal—on Sexual Choices, Family Matters, & Loss
Real Kids: The Real Deal—on Stressing Out, Addictive Behavior, Great Come backs, & Violence
Real Kids: Word on the Street
Student Underground: An Event Curriculum on the Persecuted Church
Understanding Your Teenager Video Curriculum
Youth Ministry Outside the Lines: The Dangerous Wonder of Working with Teenagers

STUDENT RESOURCES

Downloading the Bible: A Rough Guide to the New Testament
Downloading the Bible: A Rough Guide to the Old Testament
Grow For It Journal through the Scriptures
So What Am I Gonna Do With My Life? Journaling Workbook for Students
Spiritual Challenge Journal: The Next Level
Teen Devotional Bible
What (Almost) Nobody Will Tell You about Sex
What Would Jesus Do? Spiritual Challenge Journal
Wild Truth Journal for Junior Highers
Wild Truth Journal—Pictures of God
Wild Truth Journal—Pictures of God 2

SO YOU WANNA GET YOUR KIDS TALKING ABOUT REAL-LIFE ISSUES?

Then don't miss the full set of updated TalkSheets!

JUNIOR HIGH • MIDDLE SCHOOL TALKSHEETS—UPDATED!

MORE JUNIOR HIGH • MIDDLE SCHOOL TALKSHEETS—UPDATED!

JUNIOR HIGH • MIDDLE SCHOOL TALKSHEETS PSALMS & PROVERBS—UPDATED!

HIGH SCHOOL TALKSHEETS—UPDATED!

MORE HIGH SCHOOL TALKSHEETS—UPDATED!

HIGH SCHOOL TALKSHEETS PSALMS & PROVERBS—UPDATED!